BARTENDER'S
POCKET GUIDE

NEW
HOLLAND

BARTENDER'S
POCKET GUIDE

KATHY HAMLIN

First published in 2005 by New Holland Publishers
London • Cape Town • Sydney • Auckland
www.newhollandpublishers.com

86 Edgware Road, London W2 2EA, United Kingdom

80 McKenzie Street, Cape Town, 8001, South Africa

14 Aquatic Drive, Frenchs Forest, NSW 2086, Australia

218 Lake Road, Northcote, Auckland, New Zealand

ISBN 1 84330 868 1

Although the publishers have made every effort to ensure that the
information contained in this book was researched and correct
at the time of going to press, they accept no responsibility for
any inaccuracies, loss, injury or inconvenience sustained by
any person using this book as reference.

Publishing managers: Claudia dos Santos, Simon Pooley
Commissioning editor: Alfred LeMaitre
Editor: Leizel Brown
Concept and design: Christelle Marais
Production: Myrna Collins
Picture researchers: Karla Kik, Tamlyn McGeean
Proofreader: Samantha Fick

Reproduction by Hirt & Carter (Cape) Pty Ltd
Printed and bound in Singapore by Tien Wah Press (Pte) Ltd

10 9 8 7 6 5

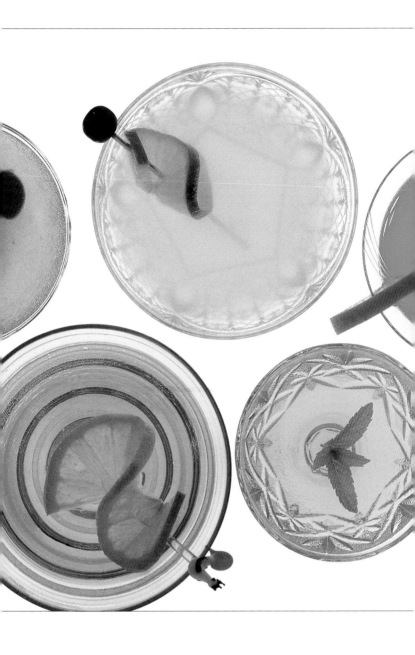

CONTENTS

The World of the
BARTENDER

INTRODUCTION

Everyone knows what the oldest profession is. I believe bartending is just as old. As long as there have been servants, people have been mixing drinks and serving them. In fact, public drinking houses date back to 2100BC in ancient Babylon. It was an important profession back then, so much so that as a penalty tavern keepers were drowned for short-shooting drinks. Today, it is still as important but fortunately, we don't suffer the same fate.

One of the very first, noted flair bartenders was 'Professor' Jerry Thomas. In 1862 he wrote *The Bon Vivant's Companion or How to Mix Drinks*, and travelled the globe hawking his book and showing off his talents as a mixologist. His Blue Blazer cocktail awed most, as he streamed an ignited concoction of Scotch, water and a tad of honey back and forth between shakers. That was the beginning of what has now become a popular craft with bartenders, trying to find their own distinct style to entertain customers. While finding your own style may not involve flaming drinks or tossing bottles and glasses into the air, there are basics you must have grasped before you can be an effective bartender, even if it's just for a small gathering of friends at home. Remember: the more you know, the easier the task. Take the time to learn a little and you will be rewarded with the impression you will make on others.

There have been many well-known bartenders over the years. An exceptional bartender is one who has a good personality and loves mixing drinks. It is the bartender's responsibility to ensure that people come back for more. This takes a certain amount of people skills, so once you know the basics of bartending you can focus on the people around you. In a home bar situation, mixing drinks for friends takes a little less effort, as the atmosphere is already set to have fun.

Bartending seems quite glamorous to some, fun to others, and just a job to a few — who probably aren't cut out for it anyway. It can certainly be any one of those, but above all it should be rewarding. Whether you intend entertaining your friends at home, doing it as a part-time job, or as a bona fide career, the main objective must be to take your position as a friend, confidant, server and mixologist seriously.

Because alcohol is a depressant, it causes different reactions in people as inebriation occurs. Body weight, medications, physical conditions and alcohol tolerance all play a part in how each person handles drinking. A first-time drinker may get absolutely silly upon having just one drink. A three-hundred-pound man may be able to tolerate ten drinks before showing any signs of drunkenness. On the other hand, this same three-hundred-pound man may react to a few drinks differently if he is under the influence of medication. The point is that you never know how a person will react and no matter how well you know a person, when serving them drinks, it is your responsibility to guard against a potentially precarious situation.

Knowledge of the craft is of utmost importance when tending bar. The purpose of this book is to make even the home bartender look like a professional, and for the professional to hone his or her skills. The first few chapters will help you set up and start to build your supplies and learn basic and advanced techniques. In the second part of this book, you will find the most current recipes available at the time of going to print, along with the old standards from classic martinis, signature drinks, shooters and holiday drinks.

Always remember this: laugh and the world laughs with you, cry and the only one listening is the bartender, but only if you are a good tipper. Enjoy!

Opposite Marlene Dietrich, here seen in the film Blonde Venus, looks like she knows all about the after effects of some enthusiastic cocktail tasting.
Below Bebe Daniels drains her drink as Julia Faye and William Boyd look on in Nice People.

TOOLS OF THE TRADE

There are only a few crucial items needed for tending bar. Many of them you probably already have in your kitchen, or you could improvise. If you are planning to purchase your bar equipment, rather go for good-quality items that will last. Bartending will probably be a more pleasurable experience if you have all the equipment – from the right glassware to something as simple as the long-handled bar spoon. We will also look at how to set up your bar, so that everything is close at hand.

GLASSWARE

1. CHAMPAGNE FLUTE

A tall, stemmed, wine-type glass that is used for champagne cocktails and creamy 'up' drinks such as the Brandy Alexander.

2. CORDIAL GLASS

Also known as a liqueur glass. The cordial glass is a small, stemmed glass used for sipping after-dinner drinks. You can also serve fruit spirits in this glass.

3. COCKTAIL GLASS

A stemmed glass with sloping sides. It is ideal for serving drinks without ice or with fruit garnishes.

4. CHAMPAGNE SAUCER

Short, stemmed glass with a wide bowl for serving champagne.

5. HIGHBALL GLASS

A tall glass for serving a drink that contains a spirit and mixer.

6. STEIN

The stein is a fancy mug that bulges at the bottom, is narrower at the top and has a handle. This mug is used for serving beers and ales.

7. SNIFTER

A balloon-shaped glass with a short stem. It is bigger at the bottom and used for sipping brandies and cognacs. It allows you to sniff the aromas of your drink for full enjoyment.

8. SCHOONER

The schooner is a tall glass that is narrower at the bottom and slightly wider at the top. It is used for various beers and ales.

9. PILSNER

This is a tall, tapered beer glass used primarily for highly carbonated, light beers and Pilsners.

10. MUG

A heavy, handled glass for serving beers and ales.

6   7   8   9   10

11. WHITE WINE GLASS

A stemmed glass with an oval-shaped bowl, used for serving white wine. It is smaller than a red wine glass.

12. RED WINE GLASS

A stemmed glass with a round bowl that tapers inward at the rim. It is used to serve red wine.

13. OLD-FASHIONED GLASS

This is a short glass with a fairly heavy base. It is used to serve whiskey and sweet vermouth, and drinks served with ice.

14. LOWBALL GLASS

A short, footed glass used to serve stirred cocktails with ice. It is also used to serve Bloody Marys and drinks that contain alcohol with a large amount of mixer.

15. SHERRY GLASS

A very short, stemmed glass used to serve after-dinner sherry. It is also perfect for serving apéritifs, ports and other dessert wines.

11
12
13
14
15

16. TULIP

Also referred to as a poco glass. It is bowl shaped at the bottom, contours in and flutes out at the top. It is used to serve wines or brandies.

17. MARGARITA

Also known as a coupette, this stemmed glass has a very narrow base that rises and opens to a large top diameter.

18. SHOT GLASS

This is also known as a whiskey glass. It holds about 45ml (1½oz)

for straight shots and can be used as a bar measure in place of a jigger.

19. HURRICANE

Shaped like a hurricane lamp, this glass was named for the Hurricane cocktail, but holds many other tropical drinks.

20. ROCKS

This glass holds a few ounces and is used to serve a drink 'on the rocks', and sometimes also to serve a shot of a spirit.

16
17
19
18
20

HANDLING GLASSWARE

Always pick up a glass near its base – a stemmed glass by its stem – and not at the top where someone will be drinking from it. This leaves the least amount of fingerprints and helps to maintain a chilled glass. When clearing away glasses, try not to pick them up by the lip because germs are easily spread. Wash your hands properly after handling dirty glasses.

Proper washing is essential to maintain sanitized and residue-free glassware. The glassware in your home bar will be sufficiently sanitized if you follow the manufacturer's directions on your dishwasher. A professional bar however, should have three sinks for washing. The first tank should hold hot water with low-suds soap, the second, hot, clear water for rinsing, and the third should contain sanitizer. Good soap products and sanitizers are commercially available.

Grab hold of glasses by the stem to avoid marking the glass or warming the drink.

Spindled brushes allow the bartender or barback to wash two glasses at a time. Twist the glasses around to reach all sides then dip them heel down into the second basin, allowing water to cover the entire inside and outside of the glass. Bring them out top down, and repeat into the third tank. Air-dry your glassware on a mat or strainer. To avoid lint or other possible residue, do not towel dry your glasses.

Store your glassware rim down in a safe place. Overhead racks are not recommended because the rise of smoke and other odours can leave a residue on glasses.

EQUIPMENT

PONY-JIGGER MEASURE

A two-sided bar measure for pouring exact quantities of ingredients for drinks. It has  a 30ml (1oz) cup at one end called a pony, and a 45–60ml (1½–2oz) cup at the other end called a jigger.

SPEED POURER

This handy little tool goes on the end of your bottle to help you pour even shots. Pourers come fitted with screens to keep fruit flies from getting into your liqueur or other spirit. They also come pre-measured, so if you have one you don't really need a jigger.

ICE SCOOP

This is an essential piece of equipment. The trick is to keep your hands off the ice to avoid any contamination – always use utensils. Never put a glass in ice, you risk breaking it. For the home bartender it is quite in order to use tongs.

COCKTAIL SHAKER

A cocktail shaker is very useful and most consider it an absolute must for the home bar. The two most popular are the Boston and European shakers. The Boston shaker consists of a metal tin, a mixing glass, and a strainer that fits over the tin. The European shaker is usually made of stainless steel and its pieces fit together for easy mixing.

STRAINER

There are two types of strainer. One fits onto the shaker and strains ice and/or fruit from your drink, the other is for your first sink – it holds the waste from your glass before you wash it.

BLENDER

The blender is used for frozen drinks. Industrial blenders can crush ice cubes, but always use shaved or crushed ice in a standard blender to prevent the motor from burning out.

PARING KNIFE

You will need a small, sharp knife for cutting and scoring fruit.

LONG-HANDLED BAR SPOON

This spoon is round at the bottom and has a long handle. You can pour

liquid down the handle to layer drinks slowly. Use the back of the spoon to float a layer on top of a drink. The long handle is the perfect tool for stirring drinks in your mixing glass.

CUTTING BOARD

A small board is used for cutting your fruit garnishes.

TOWELS

A good supply of lint-free towels is handy for wiping your hands, spills and the bar surface.

CAN OPENER

This common instrument is a must-have for any bar. The mounted type with a cap-catcher is the best to have.

CORKSCREW

Any standard corkscrew will do. There are many types, but a good waiter's corkscrew is the most professional in presentation. It folds like a pocket knife, has a small blade to remove the seal from the bottle neck, and works by prying or leveraging the cork up the bottle neck.

JUICER

For fresh juices, a hand juicer is ideal. You can squeeze as much as you need, from half a lime to dozens.

LIGHTER

Matches are fine for igniting drinks, but can drop ashes in them if you are not careful. Lighters are practical and come in handy for lighting your patrons' cigarettes.

MUDDLER

A muddler can be as simple as the back of a spoon, but the real thing is a wooden pestle used to mash fruit or herbs in your glass.

BAR SET-UP

A bar set-up depends on the size and mode of operation for each establishment. Each bartender should have his own station, which usually consists of a few key accessories.

Cocktail mats create a well for spillage when mixing and pouring drinks. They also make a neat holder for your jiggers.

A napkin holder with pockets is nice to have right where you mix your cocktails. The pockets hold your stirrers and straws for taller drinks, and the cocktail napkins are very handy to serve along with each drink.

The ice bin generally sits right in front of the bartender in his station Removable pockets or holders fit along rims on each side of the ice bin. These hold your most common mixers and also serve to keep them chilled without contaminating the ice.

Speed racks sit below your bar station and hold your stock. A good bartender will be able to pull a bottle off this rack without looking and hold exactly the one he intends to use. Various establishments have their own order

__Above__ Napkin holders keep things organized and are an essential requirement for any bar.
__Below__ You can invest in special salt and sugar rimmers, but saucers do the job as well.

for their bottles, but a good way is to start from left to right with your clear liquors, whiskies and then most used liqueurs.

A salt and sugar rimmer is very handy for rimming the tops of your glasses. These are generally foldable for easy storage when not being used, and plastic for easy cleaning. You may use saucers in place of a rimmer, but they take up more space.

THE WELL-STOCKED BAR

The well-stocked bar features a good range of basic liquors. Since most cocktails start with a base of vodka, rum, gin, blended whiskey, bourbon, Scotch, tequila and brandy, it is advisable to stock up on these. Secondary ingredients include triple sec, sweet and dry vermouth, white and dark crème de cacao, white and green crème de menthe, coffee liqueur, amaretto, peach schnapps, apricot brandy and various other liqueurs. Mixers are often used in combination with these, so you should have them readily available too.

BASIC SPIRITS

VODKA

Vodka is the purest of spirits, and is generally clear, except for the flavoured varieties. It produces less of a hangover than other spirits and goes undetected on the breath. Vodka

can be stored at room temperature, but store it in the freezer for the best taste. The proof of vodka ranges from 80 to 100 (40–50% alcohol), so it will not freeze.

It is not clear where vodka originated, but Poland and Russia are the likely candidates. The term 'vodka' is derived from the Russian word *wodka*, which means 'little water'.

Vodka is made from neutral spirits. The best ones are distilled from grain or potatoes, although any starch can be used.

Distillation occurs in pot or continuous stills. After distillation, it is diluted with water and

distilled again, or filtered through activated charcoal.

This is done to remove the congeners (chemical impurities produced during fermentation that give the spirit its colour and taste). The more vodka is rectified and filtered, the less congeners it will contain. The aim is purity. Sometimes the end product is so pure that flavours have to be put back in.

Flavoured Vodka

Contrary to popular belief, flavoured vodkas are nothing new. In fact, the earliest form of vodka, which was used for medicinal purposes, was sweetened with herbs to mask the taste of poor distillation.

The best flavoured vodkas undergo a maceration process, in which the grain is soaked for various lengths of time. The manual addition of flavouring takes place shortly before bottling.

Vodka can be flavoured with anything – from apple to vanilla. The Polish Zubrowka brand has a blade of bison grass in every bottle. Legend has it that the best grass comes from a patch where bison have urinated and that drinking it confers strength.

Another Polish vodka is Starka. Legend has it that Polish noblemen buried it in oak casks at the birth of a daughter, and drank it at her wedding. Starka is made from rye and is indeed aged – some batches up to 50 years – though ageing is not a standard requirement for vodka.

GIN

Gin, like vodka, is a pure, clear alcohol that has no taste in itself and is flavoured using a variety of herbs, called 'botanicals'. The primary flavourant is juniper berries, which lend the gin its characteristic tangy pine taste.

Gin is flavoured by one of two methods: heat mix is a redistillation process; in a cold mix the herbs and spices are steeped.

Dr Franciscus Sylvius, a 17th-century Dutch physician, is credited as being the inventor of gin. This is probably incorrect, as his was merely the first recorded distillation. His *genever* (from the French term *genièvre*, meaning juniper) was sold as a kidney tonic.

Gin became popular in England during the reign of William and Mary. When home distillation was legalized, gin became readily and cheaply available, and was favoured by the poor. Heavily sweetened to mask the taste, this brew became the forerunner of Old Tom's gin.

Dutch Gin

There are two types of Dutch gin: *oude* (old), and the lighter *jonge* (young). The terms have nothing to do with age – they denote methods of distillation. Dutch gin is not really suitable for cocktails and is often enjoyed neat.

Dry Gin

When the copper still invented by Aeneas Coffey was patented in 1830, a better, much drier gin could be produced in great quantities. This spirit, a far cry from the raw products of the numerous home stills, quickly gained acceptance among London's upper class. Known as London Dry, this gin is the most prevalent form and a key ingredient in many mixed drinks.

Wacholder

German gin is named for the *Wacholderbeere* (juniper berries) used to flavour it. Usually bottled in stoneware crocks, the popular, strongly flavoured digestive is served as a well-chilled shot, with a beer chaser or in coffee.

Golden Gin

Golden gin is the only aged gin. It is aged briefly in wooden barrels and has an attractive pale golden colour. However, it is not often used for mixed drinks.

Plymouth Gin

This spirit is made in Plymouth, England, from the waters of the Devon Moors, which are said to give this gin its characteristic softness.

Bathtub Gin

During Prohibition in the United States (1920–33), a form of gin was illegally produced – often in bathtubs, hence the name – by distilling the poisonous substances out of denatured alcohol to recover the ethyl. The product was then flavoured with juniper berries, diluted and bottled. This was a dangerous drink – if the formula was incorrect, its consumption could result in death.

RUM

Made mainly from molasses, rum is a by-product of the sugar production process. Yeast is added to most rums, but is not essential as the sugar in molasses ferments on its own. The combination of yeast, fermentation time, temperatures of distilling and the type of still used give each rum its individual flavour.

The origin of the word 'rum' is debatable. Some believe that it is the shortened form of *rumbullion*, a Devonshire word for 'uproar', others say that it stems from the Latin *saccharum* (sugar). Whatever the case may be, the fact is that this aromatic spirit enjoys worldwide popularity despite its rather disreputable beginnings.

Though rum is commonly associated with the Caribbean, cane sugar is not native to this region. It was introduced by the Spanish during the 16th century; some sources claim that Christopher Columbus planted sugar cane on Hispaniola and Cuba during his second voyage, in 1493.

Over the next two centuries, the sugar plantations of the West Indies – worked by slaves from West Africa – became key in the development of global commerce. Sugar was a cornerstone of the notorious 'triangular trade': molasses and rum exported from the Caribbean made fortunes for the plantation owners in Europe, and financed the export of manufactured goods, which were exchanged for slaves in Africa; the slave trade provided abundant cheap labour for the plantations and distilleries in the Caribbean and South America.

The Caribbean is still the centre of the industry and rum is still very big business. As a result it is often the pawn in a game that is distinguished by politicking and commercial conflict.

In 1740, Admiral Vernon, nicknamed 'Old Grog' for his habit of wearing a cloak of grogram fabric, made unwelcome changes to the neat rum issued daily to Royal Navy sailors. By adding water, lime and sugar to prevent drunkenness, he produced a mixture they scornfully dubbed 'grog'. The daily rum ration was a Royal Navy tradition that lasted until 31 July 1970, known since as Black Tot Day.

Silver or clear is the lightest of rums and best for mixing cocktails. Rum can also range from amber to dark brown. Generally, distillation takes place in pot stills for heavier and dark rums and in column stills for light rums.

Light Rums

Light rums are distilled in column stills and stored in tanks for a brief period before bottling. Some are aged up to a year and filtered before bottling. Most notable among the light and Puerto Rican rums is Bacardi, originally made in Cuba. In the 1930s, however, distilleries opened in Mexico and Puerto Rico, as the latter allowed for importation to the US without the imposition of import duties.

After Fidel Castro took power in 1959, he nationalized Cuba's rum industry. Bacardi ceased its Cuban production and Puerto Rico became the company's main distillery. Other producers of silver rums are Haiti, Mexico, Venezuela, the Virgin Islands and the Dominican Republic.

Heavy Rums

The golden rums are medium-bodied and mellower than lighter varieties. Their colour comes from the wooden barrels in which they are aged, as well as through the

addition of caramel for flavour. Añejo rums are aged for between four and seven years.

Dark Rums

Best for sipping, dark rums are often designated by a red label and their taste depends on how and where they were produced. They are distilled in pot stills and aged from five to 20 years.

Demerara rum from Guyana is named for the Demerara River that irrigates most of the sugar crops. Notable brands include Banks, El Dorado and Lemon Hart. Barbados and Haiti also produce fine rums.

France imports most of its rums from the French West Indies, with the island of Martinique being the largest producer. Many of these are made with the addition of dunder, or residue from a previous batch (comparable to sour mash).

Aromatic Rums

Aromatic rums include spiced and flavoured varieties derived from the maceration of various fruits and spices.

WHISKY

Whisky (spelled 'whiskey' in the USA and Ireland) is a spirit made from mashed, fermented grain that is distilled and diluted, and then aged in wooden barrels.

Its name comes from the Gaelic term *uisce beatha* meaning 'water of life'. It is believed that the Irish were the first producers and that Irish missionaries introduced the spirit into Europe in the fifth or sixth century. It is likely too, however, that European monks introduced whisky into Ireland. French methods of distillation seem to give credence to this possibility. Apart from that, the French term for brandy and other spirits, *eau de vie*, literally means 'water of life'.

A turning point in the history of whisky – and in the distillation of alcohol in general – came in 1830 with the patenting of the Coffey still, named after its inventor, Irishman Aeneas Coffey. The pot stills then in use meant distillation was a very slow and labour-intensive process. They required much fuel, and wastage was high. The new still enabled uninterrupted distillation, speeded up production, and meant that whisky, among other spirits, could be produced in much greater volumes.

Scotch Whisky

There are three types of Scotch whisky: malt, blended and vatted. Malt Scotch is made from water, yeast and barley. The barley is soaked and germinated, then it is dried slowly over a peat fire (which imparts the characteristic smoky flavour). Finally it is diluted, then fermented and distilled twice in pot stills.

Three areas in Scotland produce the malt varieties: the Highlands, West Highlands (particularly the island of Islay) and Lowlands. If unblended malt from one particular distillery is bottled, the product is defined as 'single malt'; each distillery is said to have its distinctive flavour. Single malts were, until recently, the preserve of the Scots, but are now enjoying increasing popularity worldwide, despite their higher price tag.

The development of the Coffey still meant that grain whisky gained enormously in popularity, as it could now be blended with neutral and other grain spirits, and be produced in greater quantity. This led to the exportation of the many lighter blended varieties of Scotch that the world has come to love.

A vatted malt whisky is a blend using secret recipes for blending different single malt whiskies that can come from anywhere in Scotland. (Although Scotch can be bottled anywhere, it must all be distilled in Scotland and aged in oak barrels for a minimum of three years.)

Irish Whiskey

Traditional Irish whiskey, made from malted as well as unmalted barley, is triple distilled using pot stills, and aged for no less than five years.

The very first licensed Irish distillery was Bushmills in County Antrim. Irish whiskey was available throughout Ireland and Britain into the 1800s. Much of it was made illegally because British excise laws prevented all but the larger distilleries from obtaining a licence to produce. Thousands of legal and illegal operations produced whiskey in pot stills until, in 1848, Britain did away with the legal restrictions governing grain imports. Grain (known as corn) could now be imported cheaply from North America, and Scottish distilleries quickly seized this opportunity.

Though grain whisky was not comparable to the original Irish product, it could be blended for improved flavour and was much cheaper, allowing scotch to gain a firmer foothold in the market.

The great potato famine in the mid-1800s reduced the market for Irish whiskey. In the 20th century, exports were curtailed by political turmoil following the 1916 Easter Rising, the subsequent civil war and a British embargo. The American market dried up with Prohibition.

By the 1960s, only a handful of distilleries were left. The Cork Jameson and Power distilleries merged in 1966, forming the Irish Distillers Group. They began producing whiskey near the Cork plant. Bushmills joined this group in the 1970s. The Irish Distillers Group is now part of the Pernod Ricard group.

Recent years have seen a resurgence of small, independent distilleries, who pride themselves on producing single malt and blended whiskey for the connoisseur.

American Whiskey

The first American whiskey was made from rye, after colonists found that the grain yielded a spicy and flavoursome spirit. This was the predecessor of bourbon.

The Scotch-Irish colonists from Pennsylvania were the first to produce bourbon. When the Continental Congress placed an unpopular excise tax on whiskey production in 1791, the colonists' refusal to pay led to the Whiskey Rebellion of 1791–94. Many of the rebels were resettled in Bourbon County, Kentucky, created through the division of Virginia in 1786. The county, named for the French royal house, became a centre for the production of whiskey, naturally dubbed 'bourbon'. Ironically, bourbon is no longer made here.

Straight bourbon must be distilled from a mash that contains at least 51% corn, and has been aged for a minimum of two years. The remainder of the mash can be corn, rye, wheat or malted barley. It must be aged in new, charred oak barrels, which are then sold to whisky producers in Canada and Scotland after use.

Blended bourbon has to be at least 51% straight bourbon, while the remainder can consist of neutral spirits or whiskey matured in used barrels.

Sour mash bourbon is a term that describes the government-regulated addition of 'backset' (stillage) to the fermentation process. This alcohol-free liquid, a residue left in the still after distillation, contains solid particles that prevent contamination by bacteria.

Contrary to what many believe, whiskies such as Jack Daniel's and George Dickel are not bourbons. Instead, they are Tennessee whiskies, a group distinguished by the process of charcoal mellowing, which takes place prior to barrelling.

Canadian Whisky

Canadian whisky is light and smooth. It is made from a mash of corn, barley and rye, and then distilled in continuous stills that produce an almost pure spirit. It is aged for a minimum of two years, though six to eight years is more customary.

Its history dates back to the 1800s when rum, prevalent at the time, was mixed with 'high wine' (a high-proof whisky spirit made from grains) to stretch it and add flavour. Fur traders realized that the Indians enjoyed 'fire-water' and it fast became an important commodity.

By the 1860s, Canadian copper stills were producing whisky by the barrel. It became a big import, especially to the United States and was a highly prized bootleg product during the Prohibition era from 1919–33.

Seagrams, one of the first to be legalized after the ban was lifted, is still one of the most popular whiskies in America today.

MEZCAL AND TEQUILA

Before the Spanish arrived in Mexico in 1519, the Aztecs were making pulque by fermenting juice from the heart (*piña*) of the agave. The Spaniards distilled pulque to improve its taste and the result was what we know as mezcal and tequila. Legend has it that it was so crude and hallucinogenic, that a larva was put into each bottle to absorb the toxins. This 'worm' was said to have aphrodisiac properties and give strength to anyone brave enough to eat it.

The difference between mezcal and tequila lies in the plants from which each is made. Mezcal can be made from any kind of agave, tequila only from the blue agave. The plants take eight to 12 years to mature. Then their *piñas* are harvested by hand and sun dried. For mezcal, layers of *piñas* are baked in holes in the ground for three to five days. For tequila, the *piñas* are cooked in stone ovens, then mashed and left to ferment. Finally the mash is distilled and bottled.

In 1978, the Mexican government established the *Norma Oficial Mexicana* (NOM) to control the quality and trade rights of export tequila (designated by NOM on the label).

These days, most of the brands are made using modern production methods. It is a treat and worth the money, therefore, to find a 'Mexican Cognac' that was produced in the traditional way.

- *Plato* or *blanco* (silver) is not aged and bottled within 60 days.
- *Dorado* (gold) usually refers to its caramel colouring.
- *Resposado* (rested) is aged for two months to one year.
- *Añejo* (aged) is aged for at least one year, but no more than five.

BRANDY

Brandy is basically distilled wine. Its name stems from the Dutch *brandewijn* (burnt wine) in fond memory of that fortuitous medieval idea to ship wine in condensed form. Burnt barrels were used to transport the cargo and you can perhaps imagine the surprise when it arrived at its destination – perfectly aged!

VS – Very Special (aged for a minimum of two and a half years)

VSOP – Very Superior Old Pale (aged for four and a half years minimum)

XO – Extra Old

Armagnac

In the southwestern corner of France, produce from Gascony vineyards is made into one of the world's finest spirits.

Traditionally, the noble Armagnac is distilled only once in a still that is called an *alambic*. No sugar is added and the barrels that are used to age the liquid for anything from 12–20 years (or more) are made from a black oak that grows in the Gascony region. The result is a 'velvet flame' (smooth but fiery) flavour.

Cognac

The roots of cognac lie in the legend of a 16th-century knight of the Cognac region who feared he'd burn in hell twice – for killing his unfaithful wife and for slaying her lover.

Apparently he decided to burn his wine twice instead and store it in the cellar. Here it was discovered some years later and the knight, still alive and much relieved, entertained in style, opening the burnt wine to celebrate. News of this spirit and its creation spread throughout the region and soon everyone was using it to turn their poor, acidic wine into choice cognac.

Cognac became synonymous with fine brandy, but in 1909, the French declared that only produce from the area immediately surrounding the town of Cognac could be called cognac.

Calvados

Normandy is home to cheese, apples, cider and Calvados, said to be the finest apple brandy in the world. In this region, Calvados is traditionally served as a digestive in the middle of the meal. It also lends itself to cooking, as an after dinner drink and – of course – for cocktails.

Aged cider is double distilled and aged for a minimum of two to three years. Though it may carry a vintage, it is sometimes blended with older Calvados during the ageing process.

Eau de vie

Eau de vie, a French term that means 'water of life', denotes a brandy that is made from the very finest of fruits.

It is hardly ever aged and thus is a clear liquid. If not bottled right away, it is kept in pottery or glass containers to preserve its clarity.

In France, three different kinds of plums are used to make this fine spirit: Mirabelle, Reine-Claude and Quetsch. Fruits such as raspberries, pears, strawberries, and blackberries among others, can also be used.

Eau de vie is best served chilled as an after-dinner drink.

Marc and Grappa

Marc, pronounced 'mar' is a strong spirit distilled from the pulp left over after grapes have been pressed to make wine. Though it is made in various locations, the best varieties are produced in Burgundy. The Italian equivalent is called Grappa.

CORDIALS AND LIQUEURS

In Europe, liqueurs have been made since medieval times, when monks steeped various herbs in spirit to produce bitter elixirs they believed could cure any number of ailments, from the common cold to insanity.

Catherine de Medici is credited with introducing liqueurs to France, when she married Henry II in 1533. Today, there are many different types of liqueurs – and quite a few of them are used in cocktail recipes.

Absinthe

A strong liqueur, absinthe is distilled with a great variety of added herbs and spices, such as anise, angelica, lemon balm, licorice and wormwood, which was said to make it hallucinogenic. Absinthe was widely banned around the turn of the 19th century.

Advocaat

Hailing from the Netherlands, this low-proof liqueur is made from brandy, egg yolks, sugar and vanilla.

Amaretto

This delicious Italian liqueur has a sweet almond flavour. Amaretto di Saronno makes the original product.

Anisette

This clear liqueur is flavoured with aniseed, and has a strong liquorice flavour.

Benedictine

Twenty-seven herbs are used to make this liqueur, the recipe was obtained from monks. Benedictine is still made according to the original formula.

Chambord

This sweet, black liqueur is produced by infusing raspberries with fine cognac, and then adding various herbs and spices and acacia honey. Dubbed France's Royal Liqueur, it is sold in a distinctive bottle.

Chartreuse

For centuries Carthusian monks have brewed their 'elixir of life' using 130 herbs and spices. Naturally green, it is also available in a lighter, sweeter yellow. Only three monks at a time are allowed to know the recipe.

Cointreau

Made from the fruits of France's Angers region, and sweet and bitter orange peels, Cointreau is a delicious clear liqueur produced according to a secret recipe in use since 1849.

Crème de Cacao

This is a cocoa and vanilla-flavoured liqueur, which comes in clear (white) or brown (dark).

Crème de Cassis

This is a dark-coloured liqueur flavoured with blackcurrants.

Crème de Banane

Yellow in colour, this is a sweet, banana-flavoured liqueur.

Crème de Menthe

Flavoured with mint, this classic liqueur is available in clear (white) and green.

Crème de Noyeaux

This is a red liqueur flavoured with almonds.

Curaçao

Flavoured with orange, curaçao comes in a variety of colours, from blue to orange and clear.

Drambuie

A sweet liqueur made from Scotch whisky, honey and herbs.

Frangelico

It is said that a hermit invented this liqueur. It is flavoured with hazelnuts, herbs and berries.

Fruit Brandies

Apricot, blackberry, cherry, peach and plum are some of the most popular flavours.

Galliano

This is a golden yellow Italian herb liqueur with a distinctive flavour.

Goldschläger

Produced in Switzerland, this cinnamon schnapps is infused with tiny flakes of 23-carat gold.

Grand Marnier

Grand Marnier is a French liqueur made from cognac and bitter orange. It is a key ingredient in the making of Crêpes Suzette.

Hpnotiq

This French liqueur is made from triple-distilled vodka mixed with cognac and blended with exotic natural fruit juices.

Irish Mist

This Irish liqueur is made with Irish whiskey and honey.

Jägermeister

A German liqueur that is made with 56 different herbs, as well as fruit, and is served ice cold.

Kahlúa

This is a dark coffee-flavoured liqueur which is produced in Mexico.

Kirsch

A clear spirit that is made from cherries.

Maraschino

A dry, clear spirit made from Marasca cherries and almond flavouring.

Melon Liqueur

Midori is the most popular brand of melon-based liqueur. It is produced in Mexico using the honeydew melon.

Ouzo

The national drink of Greece, ouzo is made with many herbs and spices, of which liquorice is the most predominant.

Sambuca

This clear Italian liqueur is made from the witch elder tree and liquorice. It is generally served neat with three coffee beans. There is a dark version with a stronger coffee flavour.

Schnapps

Apple, butterscotch, peach, peppermint, root beer and raspberry are some of the most popular flavours and are used mostly for cocktails.

Sloe Gin

Sloe gin is flavoured with a wild European plum that is the fruit of the blackthorn bush. Traditionally, sloes are pricked by the thorns they grow with, and then steeped to produce a very sweet red liqueur.

Southern Comfort

This bourbon-based liqueur has become an American classic. Southern Comfort is flavoured with vanilla, orange, citrus, herbs and cinnamon.

Tia Maria

This liqueur is made according to a secret recipe of Tia Maria, a servant of a prominent Spanish family, who was rescued during the British invasion of Jamaica in 1655. By tradition, the recipe was handed down upon the engagement of the family's eldest daughter. The only known ingredient is essence of Blue Mountain coffee beans; the rest remains a secret.

Tuaca

This sweet Italian liqueur is flavoured with fruits and vanilla.

WINE

Wine is best stored on its side, at 13°C (55°F) in a dark cellar or room – a constant cool temperature is best. Warmer conditions speed up the ageing process, while cold slows it down. Slight variations are unavoidable, but great fluctuations will cause the cork to expand and contract, letting air into the bottle.

Humidity also plays a role in proper storage. If a room is too humid, the moisture present in the air can damage the label. Low humidity, on the other hand, can dry out a cork. Red wines are served at room temperature, between 11°C and 19°C (52°F and 66°F), white wines and rosés chilled, around 5°C to 9°C (41°F and 48°F).

Asti Spumante

A sweet sparkling wine that is produced in Italy.

Beaujolais

A light, fruity red wine from the Beaujolais region of France. Many prefer it chilled.

Bordeaux

The term 'Bordeaux' covers a broad range of fine red and white blended wines made in the Bordeaux region of south-western France.

Burgundy

This area of eastern France produces choice red wines known by the same name. In fact, the word 'Burgundy' is synonymous with 'red table wine' in America.

Cabernet

Cabernet Franc and Cabernet Sauvignon are two grape varietals that are blended (with Merlot) to produce fine red wines. The Bordeaux region is famous for such blends, as is California.

Chablis

Chablis is a dry white wine that is made in the Burgundy region of France. As with Burgundy for red, the name 'Chablis' has become synonymous with 'white table wine' in America.

Champagne

Although the term is used around the world to describe sparkling white wine, only the products of the Champagne region of north-eastern France may properly be called Champagne.

Chardonnay

Probably the world's favourite white wine grape, Chardonnay is used to produce a variety of full-flavoured wine styles.

An ice bucket is an attractive solution to keeping white wine perfectly chilled.

Chenin Blanc

This white grape, grown in the Loire valley but also planted in South Africa, is used for many fine wines.

Chianti

The Tuscany region of Italy produces this superb red wine.

Ice Wine

Sweet and rich, this dessert wine is made in the Niagara region of Canada. The grapes have to freeze before they are pressed.

Liebfraumilch

The name of this popular sweet, white German wine means something like 'mother's milk'.

Marsala

Made in Sicily, this is a fortified, dark, sweet dessert wine, often used in cooking.

Merlot

Merlot is known for its softness and fruitiness. A French grape varietal, it is a key ingredient of many classic red wines, particularly from Bordeaux.

Pinot Grigio

A white wine grape, also known as Pinot Gris, Pinot Grigio yields a light crisp wine.

Pinot Noir

Wines made from Burgundian Pinot Noir grapes are said to be the ultimate red wines.

Port

Port is a popular dessert wine made by adding grape spirit to red (or white) wine.

Riesling

A white grape varietal native to Germany, Riesling yields slightly sweet, fruity white wines.

Zinfandel

Introduced in the 1850s, this is now considered to be the classic Californian red wine grape.

This selection of beers presents favourites from the US, Netherlands, UK and Belgium.

BEER

The main ingredients of beer are water, hops, malt and sugar. The fermentation process is aided by yeast. The ingredients, temperature of fermentation and duration of ageing directly influence the distinctive flavour of each beer. Lagers and ales both qualify as beer, though each has quite different tastes and characteristics and is available in a variety of colours and strengths.

Ale

Ales are made with top-fermenting yeast and ferment faster, and at higher temperatures than lagers. For that reason they tend to have a fruitier, sometimes even spicy flavour. Here are some examples:

Bitter ale – A highly hopped ale classified as 'ordinary', 'best', or the stronger 'extra special.'

Brown ale – A British-style ale that is medium to dark in colour. It is lightly hopped and flavoured with roasted and caramel malt.

Cream ale – An American-style ale that is highly carbonated and golden in colour. It is aged cold.

India pale ale – Originally, this was made in England for shipment to troops stationed in India. It is highly hopped.

Lambic – This Belgian-style wheat ale is made from wild yeast and ferments spontaneously.

Pale ale – Light amber to darker in colour, this ale is full-bodied and generally on the bitter side.

Porter – English in origin, this dark, strong ale is made from roasted, unmalted barley. It is fairly heavy in body and has a slightly sweet malt taste.

Stout – Like porter, this dark beer is made from roasted malt. There are two types: dry and sweet. The most famous is the Irish dry stout, Guinness.

Wheat beer – The chief ingredient of these bottle-conditioned beers is malted wheat. A wide variety of wheat beer is available on the market.

One of the brands of ale produced in the US.

Lager

Unlike ale, lager is made with bottom-fermenting yeast. The colder fermentation temperatures decrease the amount of esters, resulting in a cleaner, smoother beer. Lagers are generally lower in alcohol content than ales.

or dark (roasted malt). Doppelbock is stronger than regular bock.

Hefeweizen – *Hefe* is the German term for yeast. This type of beer is sedimented and bottle-conditioned.

Märzen – Amber to red in colour, this German-style lager is made from hops only, entirely without sugar. It was originally brewed in March (*März*) and held through the summer months until September, or October. Marzen is the official beer served at the Oktoberfest in Munich.

These popular lagers are produced in many countries and enjoyed worldwide. Pilsner Urquell is the original Pilsner.

Here are some examples:

Bock – This is a seasonal lager, generally brewed from Christmas to May. A strong beer, it can be pale (made from dried malt),

Pilsner – The original Pilsner hails from the Czech Republic town, Pilsen, where it was brewed: in 1842 local brewers discovered that cold storage improved the taste of their beer. Today the term is used loosely to describe beer that is dry, and golden in colour.

MIXERS

Mixers dilute or enhance many different cocktail recipes. Here is a list of common mixers:

Apple Juice
Bitters
Club Soda
Coffee
Cola
Cream of Coconut
Cranberry Juice
Espresso
Ginger Ale
Grapefruit Juice
Grenadine
Half & Half
Lemon Juice
Lemon-lime Soda
Milk
Orange Juice
Passion Fruit Syrup
Pineapple Juice
Simple Syrup
Soda Water
Sour Mix
Tomato Juice
Tonic

PIÑA COLADA MIX RECIPE

425ml (15oz) cream of coconut

3 x 310ml (11oz) pineapple juice

Pour the ingredients together in a shaker and shake well. Store tightly covered in a refrigerator.

SOUR MIX RECIPE

1 egg white

2 cups water

1 cup sugar

2 cups fresh lemon juice

Whisk the egg white until it is light and frothy. Add water, sugar and the freshly squeezed lemon juice. Mix until the sugar is dissolved. Funnel into a bottle and keep refrigerated. This will last four to five days.

SIMPLE SYRUP RECIPE

Using a 2:1 ratio of sugar to water, bring the ingredients to a boil and simmer over a low heat until the sugar has dissolved. Cool and bottle. This will last for a long time if refrigerated.

The Sangrita is a refreshing drink with a distinct bite that is very popular in Mexico.

SANGRITA RECIPE

2 cups tomato juice

1 cup orange juice

¼ cup lime juice

2 tsp hot sauce (Tabasco)

2 tsp minced onion

2 tsp Worcestershire sauce

Cracked pepper, celery salt and salt to taste

Shake well, strain and refrigerate. For a more adventurous option, alternate sips of Sangrita with sips of neat Tequila. Ay Caramba!

A WORD ABOUT ICE

You can refresh a drink using the same glass, usually when a certain spirit is served 'on the rocks' and the patron hands you the same glass to refill. The rule of thumb is: always use fresh ice! When you're shaking a drink, do so with ice. Professionals would then strain the chilled mixture into a glass containing fresh ice. For home bartenders whose ice supply is limited it is acceptable to empty the contents – ice and all – into a glass.

Here are some more icy points to remember:

- Always ensure you use clean, fresh ice.
- Use a scoop to serve.
- Never put a glass on ice. If it breaks your entire stock of ice will have to be discarded.
- Never pour drinks directly over your ice supply. If you spill you'll contaminate the ice.

BASIC TECHNIQUES

The methods of mixing cocktails and drinks aren't as varied as the many spirits that go into making them, but they are essential for creating the desired drink. Some drinks require a combination of mixing techniques. The simplest ranges from pouring a shot to mixing a drink with ice in a highball glass; more complex techniques involve layering as in a Pousse Café or igniting a drink like a Flaming Lamborghini.

BLEND

A blended cocktail is either made with ice or ice cream. An electric blender with crushed ice, or a commercial processor, which will automatically crush ice, is used.

BUILD

To build a cocktail, scoop ice into a glass, pour in the spirit and then add the mixer. The drink is served with a swizzle stick for stirring.

FLOAT

To float or top is to gently pour a spirit on top of the finished drink.

FRAPPÉ

To frappé is simply to pour your spirit over crushed ice. The drink is also referred to as a mist.

SHAKE

A shaken cocktail is mixed in a cocktail shaker and then either strained into a chilled cocktail glass, or poured over fresh ice into the appropriate glass.

In the old classic movie, *The Thin Man*, William Powell plays Nick the detective, who instructs his bartender: 'The important thing is the rhythm. Always have rhythm in your shaking. Now, a Manhattan you always shake to fox-trot time; a Bronx to two-step time; a dry martini you always shake to waltz time.'

STIR

When a cocktail is stirred, it is mixed with ice in the glass-end of a Boston shaker or beaker, and stirred with a cocktail spoon. It is either strained into a chilled cocktail glass, or over fresh ice in the appropriate glass.

LAYER

Layering is a delicate process. Since each spirit has its own weight, or density, experimentation is necessary in determining the visual outcome of a layered drink. See the basic densities chart (page 249). There are two methods, both using a bar spoon: one is to pour down its twisted handle, the other is to invert the spoon and pour over its back into the glass.

MIST

There is a method of misting that is done with an atomizer. Before a drink is strained into the glass, the inside of the glass is coated with a spirit. For drier martinis, vermouth is used – the minimum of spirits is needed, but it must be equally distributed around the glass.

MUDDLE

The term 'muddling' basically means mashing. Some recipes require that herbs and fruit be

This shot of French Fire (left) and Angel's Tit (right) are good examples of expert layering.

muddled. A wooden or ceramic pestle is best, but you can also use the back of a bar spoon. Generally, muddling is done before ice and ingredients are added. The pulp is distributed around the inside of the glass.

OPENING AND POURING

SPIRITS

Bottled spirits are sealed with a tab of plastic, wax or a metal part of the cap that has to be removed before the bottle can be opened. Air is a natural enemy of spirits and once a bottle is opened oxidation occurs. This is detected by discolouration or an

This speed pourer will allow you to pour even shots with little or no spillage.

inferior taste. If you are going to use the spirit commercially or in quantity, place a pourer on the bottle – if not, replace the cap.

Fruit flies can be a very pesky nuisance as they are especially attracted to sweet spirits. A good rule of thumb is: if the spirit was bottled with a cork cap, recork it after opening.

The best method for pouring spirits is with a spout or pourer. This allows for the least spillage. For accuracy, use a jigger or a premeasured pour spout.

A more experienced bartender should be able to pour a perfect shot without the use of a jigger. This is done by count method. (The actual counts for measuring depend on how fast you count.) Different pour spouts will vary the dispensing as well, so try to stick to the same type and make sure that they are cleaned often to remove any residue that has formed by crystallization.

WINE AND CHAMPAGNE

To open a bottle of wine or champagne you will need a clean towel or napkin. If you're serving, cradle the bottle in your arm (with a napkin draped over your arm) and present the wine to the person who ordered it. Once approval is given that it is the correct bottle, continue with the opening process.

To pour champagne, pour enough so that the foam reaches the top. Once it has settled, slowly pour more to fill the glass. Once filled, twist the bottle as you bring it up to stop pouring. This action is meant to prevent spilling on the table, or worse, on the lap of a guest.

Wine

Using a knife, remove the foil by cutting just under the lip of the bottle. Wipe the mouth of the bottle clean and insert the tip of the corkscrew as close to the centre of the cork as possible. Twist the corkscrew, not the bottle, until

Champagne

Remove the foil covering from the top and undo the wire around the cork. Place the towel loosely around the neck and body of the bottle. Holding the cork with your thumb and pointing the bottle at a 45° angle away from yourself and any other person, gently twist the bottle, not the cork. The cork should ease out and be caught in the towel. Gently wipe the neck inside and out to remove any tiny pieces of cork.

Above Practise opening wine bottles so that you don't fumble or spill.
Right Corkscrews are an essential bartending tool.

you've almost reached the bottom of the cork. Using leverage, not strength, the cork should come out in a smooth and continuous motion. Wipe the bottle again to remove any tiny pieces of cork.

To pour, start with the person who ordered the bottle. Pour a small amount for sampling. If it meets with approval continue to the right, pouring (about half a glass) gently into the centre of each glass and ending with the host. Set the bottle to the right of the host either on the table if it is a red wine, or in an ice bucket filled with ice and water by the host's side. Tie or drape the napkin around the neck of the bottle.

BEER

When pouring a beer, start by pouring down the tilted side of the glass. When it is about half full, straighten it up and pour into the middle of the glass. This should give you the proper head on your beer.

Top To pour a delicate lager, like a pilsner, begin by tilting the glass at an angle.

Centre Pour the beer in a steady stream, decreasing the tilt of the glass as you pour.

Bottom Finish with the glass upright and allow the head to rise slightly above the rim.

SERVING COCKTAILS

Choose the appropriate glass for each cocktail – it is imperative that glassware is clean, streak-free and handled properly (see Handling Glassware, page 19).

Glasses should also be cold. If a drink is made on the rocks, the addition of ice before pouring the drink in the glass is sufficient. However, if a drink is served without ice, you can frost the glass. Frosting is as simple as putting glassware in a freezer for a short time, or refrigerating it for a longer period. Alternatively, put ice into a glass while preparing the cocktail, then discard the ice before pouring the drink. It won't be as cold as the other methods, but will do in a pinch. Handle glasses by the stem to avoid warming the drink with your fingers.

When you are serving, please remember 'ladies first'! This isn't always possible when people are seated around a large table, however. In this case, it is okay to follow the seating order.

Always place the drink in front of the person, and on a cocktail napkin or coaster. Etiquette in serving drinks is the same as serving food: you serve from the right and take from the left.

GARNISHING

Garnish enhances a cocktail. It can be anything from a slice of fruit or piece of candy to a swizzle stick. Some drinks call for traditional garnish, such as fresh mint sprigs for a Mint Julep, while others can be left up to your imagination and creativity.

The most common garnish is maraschino cherries. They are so versatile that they accompany many drinks, and their delicious juice can be used as sweetener in 'kiddy' cocktails.

Celery stalks and a lime wedge are used in a Bloody Mary. Other accompaniments include, but are not limited to, dilled green beans, peppers, olives, shrimp, mushrooms and pickles. Bloody Mary bars have become quite popular for brunches and home parties, where everyone can participate in creating their own perfect munch drink.

Olives are almost everyone's favourite. They are a must in most martinis and also go well with a Bloody Mary. The most common are pimento-stuffed olives, but more exotic stuffings are making there way into the neomartini world.

Whipped cream is another necessity, especially for frozen and coffee drinks. A dollop on top of your drink sets off those sweet flavours.

Other garnishes are up to your imagination. The trick is to pair the flavourings of drink and garnish. Chocolate and chocolate syrup can add a lovely touch. For a chocolate-flavoured drink, try drizzling some chocolate syrup into the glass, or sprinkle a few chocolate shavings on top. Toasted coconut, too, is a good addition, especially on top of a Piña Colada.

For this Chocolate Martini, the top of the glass is rimmed with chocolate syrup.

Umbrellas

Everyone loves a tiny paper umbrella on a tropical drink, but a word of caution: these decorations are not water-resistant. Their colour will run if they get wet, and ruin the drink.

Frosting

Some recipes call for a sugar-frosted or salt-rimmed glass. Depending on the drink, you can dip the rim of the glass in liquid, such as water or sour mix, or take a wedge of fruit and use it to wet the lip of the glass. Next, you dip the upturned glass into a saucer or commercial rimmer filled with salt or sugar. Many different colours and flavours of salt and sugar are available.

Twists

Many people confuse a twist with a wedge or wheel. A twist uses only the rind of a citrus fruit.

For a twist, first cut the ends off a washed fruit. Then, with a sharp knife, cut into the rind but not the pulp. (You can roll the fruit first to separate the layers, but with more experience you'll be able to judge how far to cut.) Continue slicing all the way around the fruit, then simply peel off a piece. The proper way to use this garnish is to encircle your glass with the rind side and then twist the peel over the finished drink and drop it into the glass. In the case of an orange, you can also light it, while squeezing the peel over the glass, for a dazzling effect.

Wedges

A wedge is a half slice of fruit. First cut the ends off a washed fruit, then slice it lengthwise and turn it over, pulp side up. Make a slit lengthwise down the centre, being careful not to cut into the rind. Turn it back over and slice it widthwise. This creates a nice half slice already prepared to sit on the side of the glass.

Wheels

A wheel is a round slice of fruit. To cut it, first cut the ends off a washed fruit, then score it lengthwise half the way through. Cut slices and you will end up with a perfectly round slice of fruit to hang on the glass.

Flags

A flag is skewered fruit. The most typical is a maraschino cherry on an orange wedge. Pineapple or other fresh fruit may also be used according to what drink you are making and what is in season.

ADVANCED TECHNIQUES

O nce you've mastered the basics, you might want to take your skills to a whole new level. This chapter introduces you to some advance techniques such as flair bartending, and party and event management. Another section covers ethics and the responsibilities of a good bartender. Although flipping and spinning bottles may sound like fun, you should always exercise caution to ensure your and everyone else's safety.

FLAIR BARTENDING

Flair bartending is all about entertaining the crowd – keeping your bar patrons happy and amused, while still maintaining excellent service. Being able to spin bottles is not what makes a great bartender, good service is far more important. No-one wants to wait for a drink, no matter how good the show. But if you have extra help or the time to entertain, then show off your skills by all means.

Flairing requires balance and hand strength. If you can juggle, you can spin and flip bottles. As with most things, practice makes perfect. Just remember that it isn't wise to practise while you're working. As you become comfortable with your ability, you can add more spins and turns. Buy a video, take a class, or just add your own style.

Remember, you can juggle all day long, but your main objective is to deliver a properly made cocktail spill-free and quickly.

Spinning

Spinning bottles is the minimum requirement. Start by using one bottle and passing it back and forth between your hands, grasping it by the neck and catching its body with the other hand, and vice versa. Never spin towards your customers. Once comfortable, you can add more bottles and move on to a flip.

Flipping

An easy thing to try is flipping the metal-end of a Boston shaker and catching it over the glass end to shake your drink. Another is a glass flip over your shoulder. Hold the glass behind your back in your dominant hand, then shoot it straight up as you flick it with your wrist. Catch it in front of you with the other hand.

Pouring

Pouring with one or more bottles in each hand requires a degree of mental skill. You must know your recipe and be able to count the different measures simultaneously. If you are a total novice, start with plastic bottles filled with various levels of water. Practise holding two or three of them by the neck between your fingers in each hand. This will increase your finger strength and dexterity.

This bartender shows off his pouring skills, which probably took some practice.

PARTY MANAGEMENT

Unless you know the tastes of the crowd you will be serving, or have only a limited menu of cocktails to serve, it is difficult to completely fail-proof your basic stock. Some people prefer wine and beer to cocktails. The best rule is to have more stock than you need, rather than too little. You can estimate three drinks per

person within the first two hours of a party. After that, a good calculation is one drink per hour per person if a meal is served. If it is a cocktail party with only hors d'oeuvres you can estimate around one-and-a-half times that amount after the first two hours. Some will drink more, others less. This is just a rough gauge.

Open bar

An open bar means that the host will pick up the tab for all the drinks his or her guests had at the event. You can expect to serve fancier and more expensive drinks at this type of bar.

Cash bar

With a cash bar arrangement the guests pay for their own drinks. Often a host will opt for an hour or two of 'open' bar, during which he or she pays, followed by cash for the rest of the event. It is not at all uncommon for one of the guests to 'open' the bar for a short period of time.

ETHICS AND RESPONSIBILITIES

The bartender's role is a sober one. In the case of the bartender, that has dual meaning.

Firstly, you must be able to assess any situation soberly and maturely. High morals and principles are vitally important. You must treat all others with respect, no matter what the situation may be. Conscientiously attending to your customers, mixing drinks and ringing up sales are what makes a good bartender.

63

Secondly, it is imperative that you remain sober and drug-free while you fulfil your duties as a bartender. You are in control of other people's sobriety and a clear head is needed at all times. People who consume alcohol usually have lowered inhibitions, which can lead to arguments. Your role as the bartender is to keep the peace and ensure that everyone is having a good time. Although this isn't always possible, it is what you should always strive for.

KATHY'S BAR

YES, HE'S HERE – FREE
HE'S ON HIS WAY – $1.00
HE'S JUST LEFT – $2.00
HAVEN'T SEEN HIM – $5.00

This amusing bar sign makes light of a darker side of pub life. Unfortunately, some people enjoy the jovial bar atmosphere so much that they forget to go home.

Attitude

Although you are working, and hard too, it should not show in your attitude. Let it be a pleasure to make those tedious layered concoctions when you are very busy, and then serve them with a smile. The patron at the bar is there to relax, unwind and have a good time. A bartender with a surly attitude is not going to be very popular, or employed for very long.

Presentation

Neatness is next to godliness for a bartender. Start your shift in neatly pressed, clean clothes. Long hair is fine as long as it is pulled back and there is no chance of getting a hair in a drink. You will be preparing and presenting with your hands, so make sure that they are well manicured. Check your breath too. Do not chew gum while you are working, but keeping some mouthwash in a back room is a good idea.

Smile

Remember that the best thing you can wear while tending bar is a smile! It is very important that you acknowledge your patrons. What you are striving for is repeat business and, hopefully, good tips.

Rules of Engagement

When a new person sits down at your bar, make eye contact and tell them you'll be with them as soon as you can, if you can't get to them right away. Now they'll know that you know they are there.

65

When you greet a patron for the first time be cordial and welcoming. Introduce yourself and if they give you their name, repeat it to help you remember it.

If you can pick up any other information about the person, or are working in a small, intimate pub, it could be good to introduce the newcomer to your other patrons. This is often remembered in a positive way.

The next time they come back, you will be able to call them by name and offer them the same drink they had the first time.

Now, should this patron come in with someone else, you must exercise caution and good judgment. The patron may not want it known that he or she has been in your bar before.

Until you really get to know someone, don't ask personal questions, especially in front of others. You never know whether they happen to be making a clandestine visit.

The confidant

Trust is paramount! People come into a bar, who actually tell their woes to the bartender. It is your honour to ensure that nothing that has been confided to you, goes any further.

You may have seen a man in with another man's wife, but it is none of your business, no matter how juicy the gossip may be. You may overhear some people gossiping about another patron. Unless you know the statements to be totally false, it is best to steer clear of the conversation and not let yourself be drawn in for comment. Try to avoid such situations altogether! An excellent tactic to extricate yourself from perilous conversations is to state – politely but firmly – that it is not your business to talk about other people's personal affairs.

The last call

The 'last call' means just that: once you've served your last drinks, don't make any exceptions or you'll be serving everyone. Know the legalities of your establishment and principality. If you serve after hours, you stand the chance of losing your licence or risk being fined.

Setting up for the next shift is your responsibility. Make sure you have restocked, have back-up wines readily available and have refilled the ice bins. The glasses should all be washed and the bar should be wiped clean. If the place is not fully equipped for the oncoming shift it is your responsibility to stay and get them into gear.

Dealing with drunks

As a bartender, it is your responsibility to not serve anyone who is too young to drink, and to keep an eye on those who are hitting the bottle a little too hard.

Signs of advanced inebriation include: spilling, excessive talking with the hands, people repeating themselves or slurring their words, lighting up two cigarettes at a time, bragging or using foul language. They may stagger and look for the next drink before they are done with the one they already have. They may even ask you to make the drinks stronger.

It is a bartender's prerogative to shut someone off. You have the right to refuse your service. Sometimes it isn't possible to spot someone who has been drinking too much until it is too late. Don't try to reason with patrons who are over their limit. Keep your conversation light and friendly, but remain firm in your decision not to serve this person anymore. Offer them food or any nonalcoholic drink instead. Contrary to common belief, coffee is not a good choice, as it can cause further dehydration and produces a more 'wide-awake' drunk.

If a person falls to the floor, passes out or becomes unresponsive, watch for signs of breathing and call for emergency help.

It is common courtesy to clean up for the next shift; the favour will be returned.

THE HOME BAR

Setting up a home bar can be as easy as setting up a card table, or as complex as installing refrigeration units and building a permanent structure. If you are planning a one-time bar for a party you can get by with a simple set-up and a limited menu. More complex home bars will vary, depending on you and your friends' tastes. It is always great fun to host theme parties, because it gives you an opportunity to decorate your home bar differently each time.

THE ONE-TIME BAR

Setting up a temporary bar for a one-time occasion is dependent on your available space and budget. Set a table in an appropriate spot that offers easy access in and out for one person, or invest in a low cost bar with bar stools. These are moveable and a good choice if you don't plan on having a permanent bar set-up. A spare room, cosy den, basement, corner in the living room, or even your garage are all good choices for setting up a temporary bar.

Preparations

Think carefully about what you'll need and prepare a list. The bare essentials will be cocktail napkins, straws, swizzle sticks, and plastic glassware if you don't plan on using your own. Unless your tea towels are in good condition, invest in some attractive new ones to wipe up spills. You may want to think of getting some decorations.

Setting up

Set up the table with a folded towel in the middle on which to prepare your cocktails, close to where the bartender will be standing. If you don't have an ice bucket, any clean, neat-looking container will do.

Depending on whether you are left- or right-handed, position a container holding straws, swizzle sticks and the napkins in front, just off to the side of your weaker hand. Place the bottles you will be using most to the side of your dominant hand, with the mixers either in front or back. Keep the tallest bottles in the back for easy access and to prevent knocking over other bottles or cans as you reach for them.

Set coolers with ice under or behind the table. You can also set another cooler with beer near the bar for guests to help themselves. If you have a shelf behind the table, it can serve as a back bar to hold back-up supplies and empty bottles.

A PERMANENT BAR

If you can afford to install a permanent bar, there are a few things to consider. Electricity and plumbing are things to bear in mind – you will want to plug in a blender and a coffee machine, as well as lights. Refrigeration units, from a 'kegerator' that dispenses cold draught beer to an actual refrigerator to keep cans chilled, require additional outlets and space. If you don't want to drain your dissolved ice into a bucket then you must consider a drain system. This will also be fundamental if you install a sink to wash glassware.

Above & left Bar memorabilia should be chosen carefully to enhance your theme. Almost everything, from pourers to glasses, can complement your choice.

Below From the 1920s through the 1950s, bartenders used chrome or silver barware, which was very popular back then.

Location

Placement of your bar is a very important part of your planning, because once it is in – that's it. You want a place where there is room enough to sit, both behind and in front of the bar, but also to move about. You may want an intimate little bar where guests can congregate, or a more open-plan arrangement where they can get a drink then move away from the bar area.

If you'll be partying in the bar area you need to allow enough space. Consider adding a small table or two, especially if you are setting up in a game room.

Decoration

Once you have decided on your type of bar, setting and mood should be considered – lighting and sound are vital.

Keep in mind that bright light is a no-no. Select light that is conducive to your theme. A decent sound system is a must.

For a one-time bar simple party decorations are in order. A permanent one should to be themed. All your funny posters and plaques are appropriate if they reflect your personality.

A 'Bottoms Up' cocktail shaker and tumblers from the 1900s. The tumblers can only stand on their rims because of their rounded bottoms, hence the name.

Themed bars

Many home bars are based on a favourite sports team and decorated in the relevant colours. Some are decorated to show the owner's profession – a carpenter may have the ends of handsaws as handrails for the bar, or a fireman may have a hydrant set in a corner, or made into an ashtray.

Some bars feature a specific spirit. For example, in a bar that is based on tequila, cacti and Mexican décor would be good.

An outstanding idea is a themed bar based on cocktail memorabilia. Cocktail shakers from days gone by as well as old glassware, bottles and other collectibles are much fun to find and collect. But beware: this type of bar collection can become addictive and expensive.

Tiki bars are quite the vogue in recent years, especially if you have a pool. Your cabana, lanai or poolside will work for this type of theme. You will want bamboo or teak-carved accents added to your bar, and lots of torches and thatched palm fronds. A carved totem will give your bar that special island flair. These days, African influence is also quite popular as a choice of décor. Imagination is key!

MENEHUNE JUICE

60ml (2oz) light rum

15ml (½oz) Rock Candy syrup

15ml (½oz) orgeat syrup

1 fresh lime

ice

sprig of mint

Squeeze the juice of the lime over the ice and add the remaining ingredients with shaved ice. Shake and serve in a double old-fashioned glass. Garnish with half of the lime shell, a sprig of mint and a small menehune replica.

Menehunes are tiny gods of Polynesia. They are usually naked, but their long hair covers them. They possess many powers and are said to be quite mischievous. Trader Vic said, 'You can't see or talk to a menehune until you drink some Menehune Juice. So drink some!'

HOME PARTIES

Cocktail parties can be held even in the most modest of home bars and any occasion is an excuse to celebrate!

A fête is held in honor of someone. It may be an engagement party, a promotion or even a birthday. A soiree is an elegant event that calls for jacket and tie for the gents and evening gowns for the ladies.

The common cocktail party includes 12–30 guests. Try to keep it centered in one or two rooms from which most of the

Everybody loves an occasion to dress up! You can hire costumes from specialist outlets or design your own flamboyant outfit.

chairs have been removed (to keep guests mingling). Finger foods are passed around on trays or served buffet style.

Themed parties are always popular and you can give free reign to your imagination! You can theme even the minutest detail, from your party invitations to the decorations used for your cocktails. Above all, have fun!

Cocktails

Martinis

Apéritifs

Shooters

Holidays and Occasions

Frozen Drinks

Hot Drinks

Mocktails

THE RECIPES

COCKTAILS

The term 'cocktail' has many stories behind it and one could probably argue all day long as to its derivation. My favourite story dates back to the American Revolutionary War, where a barmaid in Hall's Corners, New York named Betsy Flannigan served Betsy's Bracers to American and French soldiers. At one party with stolen English pheasants, they toasted 'Here's to the divine liquor that is as delicious to the palate, as the cock's tails are beautiful to the eye.' To which a French officer replied, 'Vive le cocktail!'

The same qualities of the cocktail are essential today — it should please all the senses. Not only must it look good, it must be pleasing to the palate, not aromatically over-powering, feel icy cold and sound tantalizing. *Vive le cocktail*, indeed!

PEARL NECKLACE

Equal parts of vodka and white crème de cacao

1 splash half and half

ice cubes

Shake the ingredients with ice and strain into a chilled cocktail glass.

WHISKEY FLIP

45ml (1½ oz) whiskey

2 tsp half and half

1 tsp powdered sugar

1 egg

ice cubes

Garnish: ground nutmeg

Shake the ingredients with ice and strain into a highball glass. Garnish with a sprinkle of nutmeg.

BLOODY CAESAR

salt and pepper

2 dashes Worcestershire sauce

2 dashes Tabasco sauce

2 dashes lime juice

45ml (1½ oz) vodka

Clamato juice

ice cubes

Garnish: celery stick and lime wedge

Build the ingredients over ice in a tall glass. Start with the spices, add the vodka and top up with the Clamato juice. Stir and garnish with the celery stick and lime wedge.

JAMAICA ME CRAZY

15ml (½ oz) amber rum

15ml (½ oz) Tia Maria

1 splash pineapple juice

ice cubes

Build over ice in a highball glass.

BLACK RUSSIAN

45ml (1½ oz) vodka

22ml (¾ oz) Kahlúa

ice cubes

Build over ice in a rocks glass.

TOOTSIE ROLL

37ml (1¼oz) dark crème de cacao

1 splash orange juice

1 splash half and half

ice cubes

Shake the ingredients with ice and strain into a chilled cocktail glass or build over ice in a rocks glass.

WINE COOLER

wine (of your choice)

lemon-lime soda (to fill)

ice cubes

Garnish: twist of lemon

Fill a Collins glass with ice, pour it half-full with wine and top up with soda. Garnish with the twist of lemon.

ABBEY COCKTAIL

45ml (1½oz) gin

1 dash orange bitters

1 splash orange juice

ice cubes

Garnish: maraschino cherry

Shake the ingredients with ice and strain into a chilled cocktail glass. Garnish with the cherry.

MALIBU ITALIAN SURFER

30ml (1oz) Malibu

15ml (½oz) Di Saronno amaretto

1 splash cranberry juice

1 splash pineapple juice

ice cubes

Build over ice in a highball glass.

PEACH BUNNY

22ml (¾oz) peach brandy

22ml (¾oz) white crème de cacao

1 splash half and half

ice cubes

Shake the ingredients with ice and strain into a chilled cocktail glass.

SLOE GIN FIZZ

37ml (1¼oz) sloe gin

1 splash sour mix

1 splash club soda

ice cubes

Garnish: orange wheel and maraschino cherry

Shake the ingredients with ice and strain into an ice-filled Collins glass. Add the splash of soda. Garnish with a flag.

SINGAPORE SLING

37ml (1¼oz) gin
1 dash grenadine
1 splash sour mix
1 splash club soda
cherry brandy
ice cubes
Garnish: orange wheel and maraschino cherry

Shake the gin, grenadine and sour mix with ice and strain into an ice-filled Collins glass. Add the splash of soda. Float the cherry brandy on top. Garnish with a flag.

Singapore Sling

VETERAN

60ml (2oz) dark rum
15ml (½oz) cherry brandy
ice cubes

Build the ingredients over ice in an old-fashioned glass.

PMF

22ml (¾oz) Chambord
22ml (¾oz) Southern Comfort
22ml (¾oz) vodka
1 splash sour mix
ice cubes

Shake the ingredients with ice and strain into a chilled cocktail glass, or over ice in a highball glass.

YELLOW FEVER

45ml (1½oz) vodka
lemonade (to fill)
ice cubes
Garnish: lemon wedge

Build over ice in a Collins or highball glass. Garnish with the lemon wedge.

ABERDEEN ANGUS

60ml (2oz) Scotch

30ml (1oz) Drambuie (heated)

1 dash honey

1 splash lime juice

Combine the Scotch, honey and lime juice in a mug. Add the heated Drambuie, stir and serve immediately.

WHISKEY SOUR

45ml (1½oz) whiskey

1 splash sour mix

ice cubes

Garnish: orange wheel and maraschino cherry

Shake the ingredients with ice and strain into a flute or sour glass, or over fresh ice in a highball glass. Garnish with a flag.

RASPBERRY SCREAMER

30ml (1oz) Chambord

30ml (1oz) vodka

1 splash orange juice

1 splash pineapple juice

ice cubes

Shake the ingredients with ice and strain into a chilled cocktail glass, or over ice in a highball glass.

COPPERTONE PUNCH

Equal parts of Midori, coconut rum and crème de banane

1 splash pineapple juice

ice cubes

Shake the ingredients with ice and strain into a chilled cocktail glass, or serve on the rocks in a high-ball glass.

MIMOSA

orange juice

champagne (chilled) to fill

Garnish: orange wheel

In a champagne saucer or flute, fill about quarter with orange juice and top up with the champagne. Garnish with the orange wheel.

JAMAICAN PARADISE

30ml (1oz) Malibu

30ml (1oz) Myers's rum

30ml (1oz) Captain Morgan

30ml (1oz) Midori

1 splash pineapple juice

ice cubes

Shake the ingredients with ice and strain over ice into a Collins glass.

QUARTERDECK COCKTAIL

45ml (1½oz) rum

1 splash dry sherry

1 splash lime juice

ice cubes

Stir the ingredients with ice and strain into a chilled cocktail glass, or over ice in a rocks glass.

ZIPPER HEAD

30ml (1oz) lemon-lime soda

30ml (1oz) vodka

30ml (1oz) Chambord

ice cubes

straw

Build the ingredients, in the order given, in a rocks glass over ice and serve with a straw.

BAILEY'S COMET I

22ml (¾oz) Bailey's Irish Cream

15ml (½oz) dark crème de cacao

15ml (½oz) vodka

1 splash half and half

1 splash club soda

ice cubes

Shake the ingredients with ice and strain into a chilled cocktail glass.

PINK SQUIRREL

30ml (1oz) crème de noyaux

22ml (¾oz) white crème de cacao

1 splash half and half

ice cubes

Garnish: walnut (optional)

Shake the ingredients with ice and strain into a champagne saucer. Garnish with the walnut, if desired.

Pink Squirrel

KENTUCKY COCKTAIL

22ml (¾oz) bourbon

45ml (1½oz) pineapple juice

ice cubes

Shake the ingredients with ice and strain into a chilled cocktail glass.

OUTRIGGER

30ml (1oz) light rum

15ml (½oz) amaretto

1 splash cranberry juice

1 splash pineapple juice

15ml (½oz) Myers's rum

ice cubes

Garnish: orange wedge and maraschino cherry

Shake all the ingredients, except the Myers's, with ice and strain into a chilled cocktail glass. Float the Myer'ss on top and garnish with a flag.

AGGRAVATION

37ml (1¼oz) Scotch

22ml (¾oz) Kahlúa

30ml (1oz) half and half

ice cubes

Build the ingredients over ice in a rocks glass.

HARVEY WALLBANGER

37ml (¼oz) vodka

orange juice (to almost fill)

Galliano

ice cubes

Build the vodka and orange juice over ice in a highball glass. Float a layer of Galliano on top. Garnish if desired.

Harvey Wallbanger

ALEXANDER

15ml (½oz) gin

15ml (½oz) white crème de cacao

60ml (2oz) half and half

ice cubes

Garnish: nutmeg

Shake the ingredients with ice and strain into a cocktail glass or champagne flute. Sprinkle a dusting of nutmeg on top.

AMBROSIA

30ml (1oz) applejack

30ml (1oz) brandy

1 dash triple sec

1 splash lemon juice

champagne (chilled) to fill

ice cubes

Shake all the ingredients, except the champagne, with ice. Pour into a chilled wine glass. Top up with the champagne and stir lightly.

RASPBERRY ZINGER

30ml (1oz) Chambord

30ml (1oz) vodka

1 splash orange juice

1 dash grenadine

ice cubes

Shake the ingredients with ice and strain into a chilled cocktail glass, or over ice in a rocks glass.

CHAMBORD SOUR

37ml (1¼oz) Chambord

1 splash sour mix

ice cubes

Garnish: orange wheel and maraschino cherry

Shake the ingredients with ice and strain into a chilled cocktail glass. Garnish with a flag.

LEANING TOWER

30ml (1oz) rum

22ml (¾oz) crème de banane

1 splash Piña Colada mix

1 dash orange juice

1 dash grenadine

ice cubes

Shake the ingredients with ice and serve over ice in a highball glass.

WHITE SPIDER

45ml (1½ oz) gin

22ml (¾ oz) white crème
de menthe

ice cubes

*Shake the ingredients with ice and
strain into a chilled cocktail glass.*

GIN BUCK

45ml (1½ oz) gin

1 dash fresh lemon juice

1 splash ginger ale

Garnish: lemon wheel

*Build over ice in a highball glass.
Garnish with the lemon wheel.*

RED DEATH

30ml (1oz) vodka

30ml (1oz) amaretto

30ml (1oz) Southern Comfort

15ml (½ oz) triple sec

15ml (½ oz) sloe gin

1 splash orange juice

1 dash lime juice

ice cubes

*Shake the ingredients with ice and
strain into a chilled cocktail glass, or
over ice in a rocks glass.*

ITALIAN MARGARITA

30ml (1oz) amaretto

15ml (½ oz) Cointreau

15ml (½ oz) tequila

60ml (2oz) fresh lime juice

ice cubes

Garnish: lime wedge

*Shake the ingredients with ice and
serve 'up' or on the rocks in a
salt-rimmed glass. Garnish with
the lime wedge.*

LYNCHBURG LEMONADE

37ml (1¼ oz) Jack Daniel's

1 splash triple sec

1 splash sour mix

lemon-lime soda (to fill)

ice cubes

*Shake all the ingredients, except the
soda, with ice and pour into a highball glass. Top up with the soda.*

JACK ROSE

45ml (1½ oz) apple brandy

1 splash lime juice

1 dash grenadine

ice cubes

*Shake the ingredients with ice and
strain into a chilled cocktail glass.*

WHITE RUSSIAN

37ml (1¼oz) vodka

30ml (1oz) Kahlúa

1 splash half and half

ice cubes

*Shake the ingredients with ice
and strain over fresh ice in a
cocktail or highball glass.*

BANANA PUNCH

30ml (1oz) rum

30ml (1oz) banana liqueur

1 splash pineapple juice

1 splash lemon-lime soda

1 splash soda water

ice cubes

Garnish: banana slices and
sprig of mint

*Shake the rum, banana liqueur and
pineapple juice with ice. Strain into
a highball glass and top up with
the sodas. Garnish with the slices
of banana and the mint sprig.*

YELLOW BIRD

30ml (1oz) rum

30ml (1oz) Galliano

30ml (1oz) crème de banane

1 splash orange juice

1 splash pineapple juice

1 dash lime juice

ice cubes

*Shake the ingredients with ice and
strain into an ice-filled Collins or
hurricane glass.*

White Russian (left) and Banana Punch

KENTUCKY COLONEL

45ml (1½oz) bourbon

15ml (½oz) Benedictine

ice cubes

Garnish: twist of lemon

Shake the ingredients with ice and strain into a chilled cocktail glass. Garnish with the twist of lemon.

SLOW SCREW

30ml (1oz) vodka

15ml (½oz) sloe gin

1 splash orange juice

ice cubes

Build over ice in a highball glass.

ULANDA COCKTAIL

45ml (1½oz) gin

22ml (¾oz) triple sec

1 dash Pernod

ice cubes

Shake the ingredients with ice and strain into a chilled cocktail glass.

WIDOW'S KISS

30ml (1oz) brandy

15ml (½oz) yellow Chartreuse

15ml (½oz) Benedictine

1 dash bitters

ice cubes

Garnish: strawberry (optional)

Shake the ingredients with ice and strain into a chilled cocktail glass. Garnish with the strawberry, if desired.

RUM NUT

30ml (1oz) rum

15ml (½oz) Kahlúa

15ml (½oz) cream of coconut

ice cubes

Shake the ingredients with ice and strain into a chilled cocktail glass or over ice in a rocks glass. Blend with ice cream for a frozen variation.

ALIEN SECRETION

Equal parts of Absolut vodka, Midori and Malibu

1 splash pineapple juice

ice cubes

Shake the ingredients with ice and strain into a chilled cocktail glass, or serve over ice in a highball glass.

THE HORSESHOE SLING

60ml (2oz) Herradura Silver
100% Blue Agave Tequila

22ml (¾oz) fresh lime juice

Benedictine, Cherry Heering
and pineapple juice to taste

champagne (chilled) to fill

Garnish: fresh fruit

*Shake all the ingredients, except the
champagne, together and strain into
an ice-filled Collins glass. Top up with
the champagne. Add the fresh fruit.*
** Created by the Regans at Cocktails
in the Country, 2003.*

SCREWBALL

37ml (1¼oz) whiskey

orange juice (to fill)

ice cubes

Build over ice in a highball glass.

APPLE BLOSSOM

45ml (1½oz) apple schnapps

1 splash cranberry juice

ice cubes

*Build on the rocks in an old-
fashioned glass.*

CAPTAIN MORGAN COOLER

30ml (1oz) Captain Morgan

60ml (2oz) pineapple juice

1 dash cherry juice

1 dash grenadine

ice cubes

*Shake the ingredients with ice and
serve in a highball glass.*

VICTORY COLLINS

37ml (1¼oz) vodka

1 splash sour mix

1 splash grape juice

ice cubes

Garnish: orange wheel

*Shake the ingredients with ice and
strain into an ice-filled Collins glass.
Garnish with the orange wheel.*

BOBBY BURNS

Equal parts of Scotch and
sweet vermouth

3 dashes Benedictine

ice cubes

Garnish: twist of lemon

*Shake the ingredients with ice and
strain into a chilled cocktail glass.
Garnish with the twist of lemon.*

DAIQUIRI

37ml (1¼ oz) rum

1 splash fresh lime juice

1 dash simple syrup or sour mix

ice cubes

Garnish: lime wedge or a cherry

Shake the ingredients with ice and strain into a cocktail glass or flute. Garnish as desired.

BRASS MONKEY

22ml (¾ oz) rum

22ml (¾ oz) vodka

1 splash orange juice

ice cubes

Garnish: orange wedge

Stir the ingredients with ice in a highball glass. Decorate with the orange wedge. Serve with a straw.

Daiquiri (left) and Brass Monkey

BABY'S BOTTOM

45ml (1½ oz) whiskey

15ml (½ oz) white crème de cacao

15ml (½ oz) white crème de menthe

ice cubes

Stir the ingredients with ice and strain into a chilled cocktail glass.

RITZ PICK ME UP

30ml (1oz) cognac

30ml (1oz) triple sec

120ml (4oz) orange juice

brut champagne (chilled) to fill

ice cubes

Mix the cognac, triple sec and orange juice with ice in a large goblet and fill with chilled champagne.

CLIMAX

15ml (½oz) amaretto

15ml (½oz) vodka

15ml (½oz) triple sec

15ml (½oz) white crème
de cacao

15ml (½oz) crème de banane

1 splash half and half

ice cubes

Shake the ingredients with ice and strain into a chilled cocktail glass.

SEPARATOR

37ml (1¼oz) brandy

30ml (1oz) Kahlúa

1 splash half and half

ice cubes

Shake the ingredients with ice and strain into an ice-filled highball glass.

ALAMO SPLASH

45ml (1½oz) tequila

30ml (1oz) orange juice

15ml (½oz) pineapple juice

1 splash lemon-lime soda

ice cubes

Stir the ingredients with ice, and serve in a Collins glass.

WHITE WAY COCKTAIL

45ml (1½oz) gin

22ml (¾oz) white crème
de menthe

ice cubes

Shake the ingredients with ice and strain into a chilled cocktail glass.

CAPRI

45ml (1½oz) crème de banane

45ml (1½oz) white crème
de cacao

45ml (1½oz) half and half

ice cubes

Shake the ingredients with ice and pour into an old-fashioned glass.

SHOTGUN

Equal parts of Absolut Citron,
Grand Marnier and lime juice

ice cubes

Build over ice in an old-fashioned glass or snifter.

CHAMPAGNE ROYALE

1 splash Chambord

champagne (chilled) to fill

Pour the Chambord into a champagne glass. Top up with the champagne.

ABSINTHE COCKTAIL

45ml (1½oz) absinthe, anisette
or Pernod

1 egg white

1 tsp sugar

ice cubes

Garnish: twist of lemon

Shake the ingredients with ice and strain into a chilled cocktail glass. Garnish with the twist of lemon.

ALMOND JOY

Equal parts of amaretto,
dark crème de cacao
and coconut rum

1 splash half and half

ice cubes

Shake the ingredients with ice and strain into a rocks glass.

FLAMINGO COCKTAIL

37ml (1¼oz) gin

15ml (½oz) apricot brandy

1 splash lime juice

1 dash grenadine

ice cubes

Shake the ingredients with ice and strain into a chilled cocktail glass.

AMARETTO ROSE

45ml (1½oz) amaretto

15ml (½oz) lime juice

club soda (to fill)

ice cubes

Build the amaretto and lime juice over ice in a Collins glass. Fill with soda.

CALIFORNIAN

37ml (1¼oz) vodka

1 splash grapefruit juice

1 splash orange juice

ice cubes

Build over ice in a highball glass.

WHY NOT?

30ml (1oz) apricot brandy

30ml (1oz) gin

15ml (½oz) dry vermouth

ice cubes

Shake the ingredients with ice and strain into a chilled cocktail glass.

MUDDY RIVER

30ml (1oz) Kahlúa

30ml (1oz) vodka

30ml (1oz) Bailey's Irish Cream

ice cubes

Build over ice in a large rocks glass.

PIÑA COLADA

45ml (1½oz) rum

1 splash cream of coconut

1 splash pineapple juice

ice cubes

whipped cream (optional)

Garnish: pineapple wedge (optional) and maraschino cherry

Shake with ice and strain into an ice-filled poco glass, or blend with ice for a frozen drink. Top with whipped cream, if used. Garnish with the pineapple wedge and cherry.

THE DEBONAIR COCKTAIL

30ml (1oz) Original Canton Delicate Ginger Liqueur

75ml (2½oz) Oban or Springbank single malt Scotch

ice cubes

Garnish: twist of lemon

Stir the ingredients with ice and strain into a chilled cocktail glass. Garnish with the lemon twist.

* Created by Gary & Mardee Regan.

LA FLORIDA

30ml (1oz) light rum

15ml (½oz) Italian vermouth

7ml (¼oz) white crème de cacao

1 dash orange curaçao

1 dash grenadine

1 splash lime juice

ice cubes

Garnish: twist of orange

Shake the ingredients with ice and strain into a chilled champagne saucer. Garnish with the orange twist.

Piña Colada

Comfortable Squeeze (left) and Clubman Driver

CLUBMAN DRIVER

30ml (1oz) Irish Mist

90ml (3oz) orange juice

1 dash blue curaçao

ice cubes

Garnish: orange wheel (optional)

Shake the Irish Mist and orange juice with ice. Strain into an old-fashioned or rocks glass. Using a straw, drop the blue curaçao down the sides of the glass. Garnish with the orange wheel, if used.

COMFORTABLE SQUEEZE

30ml (1oz) vodka

22 ml (¾oz) Southern Comfort

1 splash orange juice

ice cubes

Garnish: banana (optional)

Build over ice in a highball glass. Garnish with the banana, if preferred.

SLOE COMFORTABLE SQUEEZE

22ml (¾oz) sloe gin

22ml (¾oz) vodka

22ml (¾oz) Southern Comfort

1 splash orange juice

ice cubes

Garnish: orange wheel and
maraschino cherry

*Shake the ingredients with ice and
strain into an ice-filled Collins glass.
Garnish with a flag.*

SLOE COMFORTABLE SQUEEZE UP AGAINST THE WALL

22ml (¾ oz) sloe gin

22ml (¾ oz) vodka

22ml (¾ oz) Southern Comfort

22ml (¾ oz) Galliano

1 splash orange juice

ice cubes

Garnish: orange wheel and
maraschino cherry

*Shake the ingredients with ice and
strain into an ice-filled Collins glass.
Garnish with a flag.*

BLUE SKY

37ml (1¼ oz) blue curaçao

milk (to fill)

ice cubes

*Pour the curaçao over the ice into a
highball glass and top up with milk.*

KRETCHMA COCKTAIL

30ml (1oz) vodka

30ml (1oz) white crème
de cacao

15ml (½ oz) lemon juice

1 dash grenadine

ice cubes

*Shake with ice and strain into a
chilled cocktail glass.*

BARBARY COAST

15ml (½ oz) gin

15ml (½ oz) rum

15ml (½ oz) white crème
de cacao

15ml (½ oz) Scotch

15ml (½ oz) half and half

ice cubes

*Shake the ingredients with ice and
strain into a chilled cocktail glass.*

PINE CONE

30ml (1oz) Southern Comfort

30ml (1oz) amaretto

1 splash pineapple juice

ice cubes

*Shake the ingredients with ice and
strain into a chilled cocktail glass, or
over ice in a large rocks glass.*

HAVANA COCKTAIL

22ml (¾ oz) rum

37ml (1¼ oz) pineapple juice

1 dash lemon juice

ice cubes

Stir the ingredients with ice and strain into a chilled cocktail glass.

KNOCK ME DOWN

30ml (1oz) vodka

30ml (1oz) Malibu

15ml (½ oz) crème de banane

1 splash pineapple juice

1 splash cranberry juice

ice cubes

Shake the ingredients with ice and serve over fresh ice in a Collins glass.

BRANDY ALEXANDER

30ml (1oz) dark crème de cacao

30ml (1oz) brandy

1 splash half and half

Garnish: nutmeg

Shake the ingredients with ice and strain into a champagne flute. Garnish with a dusting of nutmeg.

SCARLETT O'HARA

37ml (1¼ oz) Southern Comfort

cranberry juice (to fill)

ice cubes

Garnish: lime wedge

Build over ice in highball glass. Garnish with the lime wedge.

COLORADO BULLDOG

30ml (1oz) vodka

30ml (1oz) Kahlúa

1 splash half and half

1 splash cola

ice cubes

Shake the vodka, Kahlúa and half and half with ice. Pour into a highball or tall glass and add the cola.

ENGLISH ROSE COCKTAIL

37ml (1¼ oz) gin

22ml (¾ oz) apricot brandy

22ml (¾ oz) dry vermouth

1 dash grenadine

1 drop lemon juice

ice cubes

Garnish: maraschino cherry

Shake the ingredients with ice and strain into a sugar-frosted, chilled cocktail glass. Garnish with the cherry.

SALTY DOG

37ml (1¼oz) gin or vodka

grapefruit juice

ice cubes

*Build over ice in a salt-rimmed
cocktail or highball glass.*

CONTENTS UNDER PRESSURE

45ml (1½oz) vodka

15ml (½oz) Galliano

15ml (½oz) Grand Marnier

15ml (½oz) Captain Morgan

ice cubes

Garnish: twist of lemon

Shake the ingredients with ice. Strain

Salty Dog (left) and Contents under Pressure

*the mixture into a margarita glass,
or highball glass over fresh ice.
Garnish with the twist of lemon.
* Created by Patsy Edward.*

YELLOW SUBMARINE

45ml (1½oz) rum

30ml (1oz) orange curaçao

1 splash sour mix

ice cubes

*Shake all of the ingredients with
ice and strain into an ice-filled
highball glass.*

ABSINTHE DRIP COCKTAIL

45ml (1½oz) absinthe, anisette
or Pernod

1 sugar cube

cracked ice

*Pour the liquor into a special drip
glass or and old-fashioned glass.
Place the sugar cube over the hole
of the drip spoon (or in a silver tea
strainer). Pack the spoon or strainer
with cracked ice. Once the ice has
melted, the drink is ready.*

BRAVE BULL

37ml (1¼oz) tequila

22ml (¾oz) Kahlúa

ice cubes

Garnish: twist of lemon

*Build over ice in a rocks glass.
Garnish with the twist of lemon.*

DEAUVILLE COCKTAIL

15ml (½oz) lemon juice

15ml (½oz) brandy

15ml (½oz) apple brandy

15ml (½oz) triple sec

ice cubes

*Shake the ingredients with ice and
strain into a chilled cocktail glass.*

LONG BEACH

22ml (¾oz) rum

22ml (¾oz) gin

22ml (¾oz) vodka

22ml (¾oz) tequila

22ml (¾oz) triple sec

1 splash cranberry juice

ice cubes

Garnish: lemon wedge

*Shake the ingredients with ice and
pour into hurricane glass or a large
tumbler. Garnish with the lemon
wedge.*

TWISTED LEMONADE

45ml (1½oz) strawberry vodka

1 splash sour mix

1 dash grenadine

ice cubes

Garnish: lemon wedge

*Shake the ingredients with ice and
strain into an ice-filled Collins glass.
Garnish with the lemon wedge.*

ROYAL PEACH

30ml (1oz) Crown Royal

15ml (½oz) peach schnapps

1 splash sour mix

ice cubes

Garnish: maraschino cherry

Shake the ingredients with ice and strain into a chilled cocktail glass or over ice in a rocks glass. Garnish with the cherry.

VODKA 7

37ml (1¼oz) vodka

1 splash lime juice

lemon-lime soda (to fill)

ice cubes

Garnish: lime wedge

Build the vodka and lime juice in a Collins glass filled with ice, add the lime wedge and top up with soda.

VANDERBILT COCKTAIL

45ml (1½oz) brandy

22ml (¾oz) cherry brandy

1 tsp simple syrup

2 dashes bitters

ice cubes

Stir the ingredients with ice and strain into a chilled cocktail glass.

ANTIFREEZE II

45ml (1½oz) dark rum

30ml (1oz) Midori

90ml (3oz) pineapple juice

30ml (1oz) sour mix

15ml (½oz) simple syrup

ice cubes

Shake the ingredients with ice, or blend to serve frozen. Serve in a poco or hurricane glass.

KAYTUSHA ROCKET

30ml (1oz) vodka

15ml (½oz) Kahlúa

1 splash pineapple juice

1 dash half and half

ice cubes

Shake the ingredients with ice and strain into a chilled cocktail glass.

BRUISE

60ml (2oz) Absolut Mandarin

15ml (½oz) raspberry schnapps or Chambord

15ml (½oz) blue curaçao

1 splash pineapple juice

1 splash lemon-lime soda

ice cubes

Build over ice in a tall glass.

BAY BREEZE

30ml (1oz) vodka

1 splash pineapple juice

1 splash cranberry juice

ice cubes

Build over ice in a highball glass.

COC-A-TOO

30ml (1oz) Crown Royal

22ml (¾oz) peach schnapps

1 splash orange juice

1 dash grenadine

ice cubes

Shake the ingredients with ice and strain into a chilled cocktail glass.

ICE PICK

37ml (1¼oz) vodka

1 splash iced tea

ice cubes

Garnish: lemon wedge

Build over ice in a Collins or highball glass. Garnish with the lemon wedge.

PEANUT BUTTER AND JELLY

22ml (¾oz) Bailey's Irish Cream

22ml (¾oz) Chambord

15ml (½oz) Frangelico

Build over ice in a rocks glass.

WHITE HEART

15ml (½oz) sambuca

15ml (½oz) white crème de cacao

60ml (2oz) half and half

ice cubes

Shake the ingredients with ice and strain into a chilled cocktail glass.

FLYING GRASSHOPPER

22ml (¾oz) green crème de menthe

22ml (¾oz) white crème de cacao

22ml (¾oz) vodka

ice cubes

Shake the ingredients with ice and strain into a chilled cocktail glass.

APPLE JOLLY RANCHER

30ml (1oz) apple schnapps

15ml (½oz) Absolut Citron

15ml (½oz) triple sec

1 splash sour mix

ice cubes

lemon-lime soda (to fill)

Shake the spirits and sour mix with ice. Pour into a highball glass and top up with the soda.

SHANDY

beer

lemon-lime soda (to taste)

*Pour the beer into a mug and add
the soda to taste.*

KIR ROYALE

22ml (¾ oz) crème de cassis

champagne (to fill)

Garnish: twist of lemon

*Pour the crème de cassis into the
bottom of a wine glass or champagne flute. Top up with champagne
and garnish with the twist of lemon.*

ACAPULCO

45ml (1½ oz) tequila

15ml (½ oz) triple sec

15ml (½ oz) rum

1 splash lime juice

1 splash sour mix

ice (optional)

Garnish: lime wedge

*Shake the ingredients and strain into
a rocks glass. Alternatively, build
over ice in a highball glass. Garnish
with the lime wedge.*

BERMUDA ROSE

37ml (1¼ oz) gin

7ml (¼ oz) apricot brandy

7ml (¼ oz) grenadine

ice cubes

*Shake the ingredients with ice and
strain into a chilled cocktail glass.*

LITTLE DEVIL COCKTAIL

30ml (1oz) lemon juice

22ml (¾oz) rum

22ml (¾oz) gin

1 dash triple sec

ice cubes

Shake the ingredients with ice and strain into a chilled cocktail glass.

FUZZY LOGIC

60ml (2oz) Tanqueray gin

45ml (1½oz) fresh orange juice

45ml (1½oz) peach schnapps

Benedictine (to taste)

Shake the ingredients together and strain into a chilled cocktail glass.
* Created by the Regans at Cocktails in the Country, 2002.

CALIFORNIA LEMONADE

60ml (2oz) whiskey

1 splash sour mix

1 dash grenadine

club soda (to fill)

ice cubes

Garnish: lemon wedge and maraschino cherry

Shake the ingredients with ice and strain into an ice-filled Collins glass.

Top up with the soda and garnish with the lemon wedge and cherry.

RUM RUNNER

30ml (1oz) rum

15ml (½oz) blackberry brandy

15ml (½oz) crème de banane

1 splash pineapple juice

1 splash orange juice

1 dash grenadine

1 dash Myers's rum

ice cubes

Garnish: orange wheel and maraschino cherry

Shake the ingredients with ice and strain into an ice-filled hurricane glass. Float the Myers's on top. Garnish with a flag.

GOLDEN MARGARITA

37ml (1¼oz) reposado tequila

22ml (¾oz) Grand Marnier

1 splash sour mix

1 dash lime juice

ice cubes

Garnish: lime wedge

Shake the ingredients with ice. Strain into a salt-rimmed cocktail glass. Garnish with the lime wedge.

THE INNERMOST SECRET

30ml (1oz) bourbon

30ml (1oz) Hpnotiq

15ml (½oz) triple sec

Peychaud's bitters (to taste)

Garnish: maraschino cherry

Shake the ingredients together and strain. Garnish with the cherry.

* Created by the Regans for Andrea Immer's television show, Simply Wine, 2003.

ABSOLUT STRESS

22ml (¾oz) Absolut vodka

22ml (¾oz) Malibu

7ml (¼oz) peach schnapps

1 splash cranberry juice

1 splash pineapple juice

ice cubes

Shake the ingredients with ice and serve in a highball glass with the ice cubes.

ARAWAK COCKTAIL

45ml (1½oz) Jamaican rum

45ml (1½oz) sweet sherry

1 dash bitters

ice cubes

Stir the ingredients with ice in a mixing glass and strain into a chilled cocktail glass.

TIA RUMBA

Equal parts of Tia Maria and rum

ice cubes

Garnish: coffee bean

Shake the ingredients with ice and strain into a chilled cocktail glass or build over ice in a rocks glass. Garnish with the coffee bean.

SMOOTH SCREW

15ml (½oz) Tia Maria

15ml (½oz) Myers's rum

45ml (1½oz) pineapple juice

15ml (½oz) Cockspur Barbadian rum

ice cubes

Shake the ingredients with ice and strain into an ice-filled Collins glass. Float a layer of Cockspur rum on top.

PLANTERS PUNCH

45ml (1½oz) rum
22ml (¾oz) triple sec
1 splash sour mix
1 splash pineapple juice
1 splash orange juice
1 dash grenadine
dark rum
ice cubes
Garnish: orange wheel and maraschino cherry

Shake the ingredients with ice and strain over ice into a hurricane glass. Float the dark rum on top. Garnish with a flag.

XAVIERA

15ml (½oz) amaretto
15ml (½oz) Kahlúa
15ml (½oz) triple sec
45ml (1½oz) half and half
ice cubes

Shake the ingredients with ice and strain into a chilled cocktail glass.

Cuba Libre

CUBA LIBRE

37ml (1¼oz) rum
1 splash cola
1 dash lime juice
ice cubes
Garnish: lime wedge

Build over ice in a highball glass. Garnish with the lime wedge.

B & B

Equal parts of brandy and Benedictine

Serve neat in a brandy snifter.

TOASTED ALMOND

30ml (1oz) amaretto

30ml (1oz) Kahlúa

1 large splash half and half

ice cubes

Shake the ingredients with ice and strain into an ice-filled Collins glass.

BLOODY BULL

45ml (1½oz) vodka

60ml (2oz) beef boullion

Bloody Mary mix

ice cubes

Garnish: lemon wedge and celery stick

Build over ice in a tall glass. with the stick of celery and lemon wedge.

VICIOUS SID

45ml (1½oz) light rum

15ml (½oz) Southern Comfort

15ml (½oz) triple sec

30ml (1oz) lemon juice

1 dash bitters

ice cubes

Shake the ingredients with ice and strain into a chilled old-fashioned glass.

CAPE CODDER

37ml (1¼oz) vodka

1 splash cranberry juice

1 dash lime juice (optional)

ice cubes

Garnish: lime wedge

Build over ice in a highball glass. Garnish with a lime wedge.

MALIBU CLASSIC

30ml (1oz) Malibu rum

15ml (½oz) Midori

1 splash sour mix

ice cubes

Shake the ingredients with ice. Strain into a chilled cocktail glass or over ice in a highball glass.

103

SOUTHERN SPARKLER

37ml (1¼oz) Southern Comfort

1 splash grapefruit juice

1 splash pineapple juice

1 splash club soda

ice cubes

Garnish: orange wheel and maraschino cherry

Shake the ingredients with ice and strain into an ice-filled Collins glass. Garnish with a flag.

BLUE VELVET

1 splash blue curaçao

champagne (chilled)

Pour the curaçao into a champagne flute and top up with champagne.

FROSTY COKE

Equal parts of vodka, Kahlúa and dark crème de cacao

1 splash half and half

Shake the ingredients together and pour into a large tumbler. Add a healthy splash of cola.

XANGO

45ml (1½oz) rum

15ml (½oz) triple sec

1 splash grapefruit juice

ice cubes

Shake the ingredients with ice and strain into a chilled cocktail glass.

YELLOW PARROT

22ml (¾oz) apricot brandy

22ml (¾oz) anisette

22ml (¾oz) yellow Chartreuse

ice cubes

Shake the ingredients with ice and strain into a chilled cocktail glass.

MATADOR

37ml (1¼oz) tequila

1 splash pineapple juice

1 dash fresh lime juice

ice cubes

Shake the ingredients with ice and strain into a chilled cocktail glass. Alternatively, serve with fresh ice in a highball glass.

PINK ALMOND

30ml (1oz) whiskey

22ml (¾oz) crème de noyaux

22ml (¾oz) amaretto

1 splash sour mix

ice cubes

Shake the ingredients with ice, and strain into a chilled cocktail glass or over ice in a large rocks glass.

SCOOBY SNACK

Equal parts of Midori and Malibu rum

1 splash pineapple juice

1 splash half and half, or milk

ice cubes

Shake the ingredients with ice and strain into an ice-filled Collins glass.

Between the Sheets

BETWEEN THE SHEETS

22ml (¾oz) rum

22ml (¾oz) brandy

22ml (¾oz) Cointreau

1 splash lemon juice or sour mix

ice cubes

Garnish: twist of lemon (optional)

Shake the ingredients with ice and strain into a chilled margarita glass.

BEACHCOMBER

45ml (1½oz) rum

15ml (½oz) triple sec

15ml (½oz) lime juice

ice cubes

Shake the ingredients with ice and strain into a chilled cocktail glass.

RED DEVIL

30ml (1oz) vodka

30ml (1oz) peach schnapps

30ml (1oz) Southern Comfort

15ml (½oz) triple sec

15ml (½oz) sloe gin

1 splash orange juice

1 dash grenadine

ice cubes

Shake the ingredients with ice and strain into a chilled cocktail glass or over ice in a highball glass.

BLACK NUTS

30ml (1oz) Frangelico

30ml (1oz) black sambuca

ice cubes

Build over ice in a rocks glass.

ALEXANDRA

Equal parts of Tia Maria, rum, cream and cream of coconut

ice cubes

Shake the ingredients with ice and serve 'up' in a cocktail glass, or serve on ice in a highball glass.

VERMONT VIGOUR

45ml (1½oz) gin

30ml (1oz) lemon juice

15ml (½oz) maple syrup

ice cubes

Shake the ingredients with ice and strain into a chilled cocktail glass or build over ice in a rocks glass.

AFFINITY

30ml (1oz) Scotch

15ml (½oz) sweet vermouth

15ml (½oz) dry vermouth

2 dashes bitters

ice cubes

Garnish: lemon wheel

Stir the ingredients with ice and strain into a chilled cocktail glass. Garnish with the lemon wheel.

DREAMSICLE

37ml (1¼oz) amaretto

1 splash orange juice

1 splash half and half

ice cubes

Shake the ingredients with ice and strain to serve 'up'. Alternatively, serve on the rocks, or blend with ice cream for a frozen drink.

MERRY WIDOW FIZZ

45ml (1½oz) sloe gin

1 splash sour mix

1 splash orange juice

club soda (to fill)

ice cubes

Shake all the ingredients, except the soda, with ice and strain over fresh ice into a tall glass. Top up with the soda.

VAN VLEET

90ml (3oz) rum

30ml (1oz) maple syrup

30ml (1oz) lemon juice

ice cubes

Shake the ingredients with ice and strain into a chilled old-fashioned glass.

AFTER-DINNER COCKTAIL

30ml (1oz) apricot brandy

30ml (1oz) triple sec

1 splash lime juice

ice cubes

Garnish: lime wedge

Shake the ingredients with ice and strain into a chilled cocktail glass. Garnish with the lime wedge.

GIN RICKEY

60ml (2oz) gin

30ml (1oz) fresh lime juice

1 splash club soda

ice cubes

Garnish: lime wedge

Build the gin and lime juice over ice in a highball glass and top with the soda. Garnish with the lime wedge

EAST INDIA I

45ml (1½oz) cognac

30ml (1oz) pineapple juice

15ml (½oz) orange curaçao

or triple sec

1 dash Angostura bitters

ice cubes

Shake the ingredients with ice and strain into a chilled cocktail glass.

KISS IN THE DARK

22ml (¾oz) gin

22ml (¾oz) cherry brandy

22ml (¾oz) dry vermouth

ice cubes

Shake the ingredients with ice and strain into a chilled cocktail glass.

ITALIAN SOMBRERO

37ml (1¼oz) amaretto

1 splash half and half

ice cubes

Shake the ingredients with ice and strain over ice in a highball glass.

HAWAIIAN QUALUDE

7ml (¼oz) blackberry brandy

7ml (¼oz) Southern Comfort

7ml (¼oz) vodka

7ml (¼oz) tequila

7ml (¼oz) amaretto

7ml (¼oz) Myers's rum

1 dash grenadine

1 splash orange juice

1 splash pineapple juice

1 splash sour mix

ice cubes

Shake the ingredients with ice and serve over ice in a large tumbler.

Clockwise from top: Mint Julep, Scotch Old Fashioned and Waterfall

MINT JULEP

mint leaves

1 dash simple syrup

60ml (2oz) bourbon

crushed ice

Muddle the mint leaves with the simple syrup, add 30ml (1oz) bourbon, fill with crushed ice and add the rest of the bourbon. Garnish with a sprig of fresh mint.

SCOTCH OLD FASHIONED

60ml (2oz) Scotch whiskey

1 splash simple syrup

1 dash bitters

1 splash club soda

ice cubes

Swirl the simple syrup and bitters around in a rocks glass to coat the inside of the glass. Add the ice and pour in the whiskey. Top up with the soda.

WATERFALL

45ml (1½oz) Crown Royal

22ml (¾oz) Chambord

90ml (3oz) pineapple juice

ice cubes

Shake the the ingredients with ice and serve over fresh ice in a large rocks glass.

STONE SOUR

37ml (1¼oz) whiskey or spirit of choice

1 splash orange juice

1 splash sour mix

ice cubes

Garnish: orange wheel and maraschino cherry

Shake the ingredients with ice and strain into a chilled cocktail glass or build over ice in a rocks glass. Garnish with a flag.

DOWN UNDER SNOWBALL

30ml (1oz) light rum

30ml (1oz) peach schnapps

15ml (½oz) grenadine

90ml (3oz) orange juice

ice cubes

Shake the ingredients with ice and serve in a Collins glass.

PRESTONE

22ml (¾oz) Rock and Rye

22ml (¾oz) coconut rum

22ml (¾oz) Midori

22ml (¾oz) Apple Puckers

1 splash pineapple juice

ice cubes

Shake the ingredients with ice and strain into a chilled cocktail glass or over ice in a rocks glass.

DI SARONNO SEA BREEZE

30ml (1oz) Di Saronno amaretto

30ml (1oz) Malibu rum

1 splash cranberry juice

1 splash pineapple juice

crushed ice

Build in a highball glass filled with crushed ice.

WHITE LION

45ml (1½oz) light rum

juice of ½ lemon

½ tsp grenadine

1 tsp powdered sugar

2 dashes bitters

ice cubes

Shake the ingredients with ice and strain into a chilled cocktail glass.

VALENCIA COCKTAIL

45ml (1½oz) apricot brandy

1 splash orange juice

2 dashes orange bitters

ice cubes

Shake the ingredients with ice and strain into a chilled cocktail glass.

CANADIAN COCKTAIL

45ml (1½oz) Canadian whisky

1 splash triple sec

1 dash bitters

1 tsp powdered sugar

ice cubes

Shake the ingredients with ice and strain into a chilled cocktail glass.

ELECTRIC ICED TEA

22ml (¾oz) rum

22ml (¾oz) gin

22ml (¾oz) vodka

22ml (¾oz) tequila

22ml (¾oz) blue curaçao

22ml (¾oz) sour mix

1 splash Sprite

ice cubes

Shake all the ingredients, except the Sprite, with ice and pour into a large glass. Top up with the Sprite.

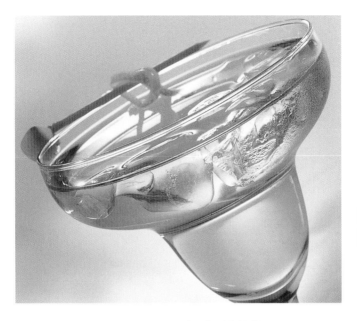

French 75

FRENCH 75

60ml (2oz) sour mix

60ml (2oz) cognac

champagne (chilled)

ice cubes

Garnish: twist of lemon

Shake the sour mix and cognac and strain into a margarita glass with just a bit of ice. Fill with champagne and decorate with the twist of lemon on a cocktail pick.

ARISE MY LOVE

1 tsp green crème de menthe

champagne (chilled)

Pour the crème de menthe into a flute and top up with the champagne.

KAPU-KAI

30ml (1oz) 151 Demerara rum

15ml (½oz) lime juice

1 splash simple syrup

ice cubes

Shake the ingredients with ice and strain into a chilled cocktail glass.

MOSCOW MULE

| 45ml (1½oz) vodka |
| 30ml (1oz) lime juice |
| ginger beer (to fill) |
| ice cubes |
| Garnish: lime wheel |

Shake the ingredients with ice and pour over fresh ice in a highball glass, or serve in a copper mug. Garnish with a lime wheel.

Moscow Mule (right) and Fruity Navel

FRUITY NAVEL

| 1 part peach schnapps |
| 1 part apricot brandy |
| 1 part orange juice |
| crushed ice |
| Garnish: maraschino cherry |

Shake the ingredients with ice and strain into a chilled cocktail glass. Garnish with the cherry.

PERFECTION

| 45ml (1½oz) whiskey |
| 1 splash club soda |
| 1 splash ginger ale |
| ice cubes |
| Garnish: twist of lemon |

Build over ice in a highball glass. Garnish with the twist of lemon.

BOCCE BALL

| 30ml (1oz) amaretto |
| 1 splash orange juice |
| 1 splash club soda (optional) |
| ice cubes |

Build the ingredients over ice in a highball glass.

HAWAIIAN COCKTAIL I

60ml (2oz) gin

15ml (½oz) orange curaçao

15ml (½oz) pineapple juice

ice cubes

Stir the ingredients with ice and strain into a chilled cocktail glass.

RUSTY NAIL

30ml (1oz) Scotch

30ml (1oz) Drambuie

ice cubes

Shake the ingredients with ice and strain into a chilled cocktail glass or build over ice in a rocks glass.

XANAX

15ml (½oz) vodka

15ml (½oz) rum

15ml (½oz) gin

15ml (½oz) 151 rum

15ml (½oz) peach schnapps

1 splash orange juice

1 splash grapefruit juice

pineapple juice

ice cubes

Shake the first seven ingredients with ice and strain into an ice-filled tumbler. Top up with the pineapple juice.

FIRE AND ICE

22ml (¾oz) sambuca

22ml (¾oz) triple sec

22ml (¾oz) brandy

ice cubes

Stir the ingredients with ice in an old-fashioned glass.

MALIBU

22ml (¾oz) spiced rum

22ml (¾oz) vodka

1 splash orange juice

ice cubes

Build over ice in a highball glass.

113

CREAMSICLE

45ml (1½oz) Grand Marnier

45ml (1½oz) Galliano

1 splash half and half

1 splash orange juice

1 dash grenadine

ice cubes

Shake the ingredients with ice and serve 'up' in a champagne glass.

VARIATION For a frozen variation, substitute the cream with ice cream and blend.

BERRY PATCH

30ml (1oz) Chambord

1 splash orange juice

1 splash cranberry juice

ice cubes

Shake the ingredients with ice. Strain into a chilled cocktail glass or build in a highball glass.

BAD HABIT

Equal parts of vodka and peach schnapps

ice cubes

Build over ice in a rocks glass.

BLUE WHALE

15ml (½oz) blue curaçao

30ml (1oz) rum

1 splash pineapple juice

ice cubes

Shake the ingredients with ice. Serve 'up' in a chilled cocktail glass, or on with ice in a rocks glass.

JACKHAMMER

37ml (1¼oz) vodka

1 splash pineapple juice

ice cubes

Build over ice in a highball glass.

FROOT LOOP

30ml (1oz) apple brandy

15ml (½oz) cherry brandy

15ml (½oz) vodka

1 splash orange juice

ice cubes

Shake the ingredients with ice and strain into a cocktail glass.

APPLE PIE

90ml (3oz) apple schnapps

1 splash cinnamon schnapps

ice cubes

Garnish: apple slice and cinnamon

Pour the schnapps over ice in an old-fashioned glass. Garnish with the slice of apple and dust with cinnamon.

STRUDLE

45ml (1½oz) cinnamon schnapps

15ml (½oz) amaretto

1 splash of apple juice

ice cubes

Garnish: cinnamon stick

Build over ice in a highball glass. Garnish with the cinnamon stick.

INCREDIBLE HULK

60ml (2oz) Hpnotiq

30ml (1oz) Hennessy cognac

ice cubes

Build the ingredients over ice in a rocks glass.

PUSHUP

37ml (1¼oz) vodka

37ml (1¼oz) orange juice

1 splash half and half

1 dash grenadine

ice cubes

Shake the ingredients with ice and strain into a chilled cocktail glass or over ice in a rocks glass. Alternatively, blend with ice cream for a tasty frozen drink.

Side Car

SIDE CAR

30ml (1oz) brandy

15ml (½oz) triple sec

1 splash sour mix

ice cubes

Shake the ingredients with ice and strain into a sugar-frosted cocktail or margarita glass; or serve over ice in a sugar-frosted highball glass.

SWISS LEMONADE

30ml (1oz) Absolut Citron

1 splash of sour mix

1 splash cranberry juice

1 splash lemon-lime soda

ice cubes

Shake the Citron and sour mix with ice, strain into an ice-filled highball glass, add the cranberry juice and top up with the soda.

GOLDEN DREAM

Golden Dream (left) and Grasshopper

30ml (1oz) Galliano

15ml (½oz) triple sec

1 splash orange juice

1 splash half and half or
a scoop of ice cream

ice cubes

*Shake the ingredients with ice and
strain into a chilled margarita glass,
or omit ice and blend with ice cream
for a frozen drink.*

GRASSHOPPER

45ml (1½oz) green crème
de menthe

45ml (1½oz) white crème
de cacao

1 splash half and half

ice cubes

Garnish: sprig of mint (optional)

*Shake the ingredients with ice and
strain into a cocktail glass or flute.
Garnish with the sprig of mint, if used.*

ITALIAN SPEAR

30ml (1oz) peppermint
schnapps

30ml (1oz) amaretto

ice cubes

Build over ice in a rocks glass.

ETHEL DUFFY COCKTAIL

22ml (¾oz) apricot brandy

22ml (¾oz) white crème
de menthe

22ml (¾oz) orange curaçao

ice cubes

*Shake the ingredients with ice and
strain into a chilled cocktail glass.*

POISON APPLE

15ml (½oz) Captain Morgan

15ml (½oz) Crown Royal

15ml (½oz) Apple Puckers

15ml (½oz) Chambord

1 splash sour mix

1 splash lemon-lime soda

ice cubes

Garnish: lemon wedge

*Shake all the ingredients, except the
soda, with ice and strain into an ice-
filled large tumbler and top up with
soda. Garnish with the lemon wedge.*

CARIBBEAN CRUISE

30ml (1oz) Myers's rum

30ml (1oz) dark rum

22ml (¾oz) Tia Maria

22ml (¾oz) cream of coconut

1 splash orange juice

1 splash pineapple juice

ice cubes

Garnish: twist of lemon

*Shake the ingredients with ice and
pour into a hurricane glass. Serve
garnished with the twist of lemon.*

BACARDI COCKTAIL

37ml (1¼oz) Bacardi rum

1 splash sour mix

1 dash grenadine

ice cubes

Garnish: lime wedge

*Shake the ingredients with ice and
serve in a chilled cocktail glass, or
serve with ice in a highball glass.
Garnish with the lime wedge.*

** The New York Supreme Court
ruled in 1936 that a Bacardi Cocktail
had to be made with Bacardi rum.*

BLACKTHORN

45ml (1½oz) sloe gin

30ml (1oz) sweet vermouth

ice cubes

Garnish: twist of lemon

Shake the ingredients with ice and strain into a chilled cocktail glass. Garnish with the lemon twist.

FLAMINGO

15ml (½oz) rum

15ml (½oz) spiced rum

15ml (½oz) Licor 43

1 splash grapefruit juice

1 splash guava nectar

ice cubes

Garnish: orange wheel and maraschino cherry

Shake the ingredients together and serve in a rocks glass, or blend with ice and serve in a poco glass. Garnish with the orange wheel and cherry.

GODMOTHER

45ml (1½oz) vodka

22ml (¾oz) amaretto

ice cubes

Build over ice in a rocks glass.

AGENT ORANGE

30ml (1oz) vodka

15ml (½oz) Grand Marnier

7ml (¼oz) triple sec

1 splash orange juice

ice cubes

Shake the ingredients with ice and serve in a highball glass over fresh ice cubes.

BANANA RUM PUNCH

30ml (1oz) rum

15ml (½oz) crème de banane

1 splash orange juice

ice cubes

Shake the ingredients with ice and strain into a rocks glass.

COLORADO MINTY DOG

45ml (1½oz) Kahlúa

15ml (½oz) peppermint schnapps

1 splash half and half

1 splash cola

ice cubes

Shake all the ingredients, except the cola, with ice. Pour into a tall glass and top up with the cola.

BACKSTREET BANGER

Equal parts of bourbon
and Bailey's Irish Cream

ice cubes

Build over ice in a rocks glass.

BLOODY MARY

pinch of salt and celery salt

1 dash Worcestershire sauce

1 dash lemon juice

2–3 drops Tabasco sauce

dusting of pepper

37ml (1¼oz) vodka

tomato juice

ice cubes

Garnish: celery stick and lime
wedge (optional)

*Build over ice in a tall glass. Start
with the spices, add the vodka, fill
with the tomato juice and stir.
Garnish with the celery stick and
lime wedge, if used.*

FOG CUTTER

60ml (2oz) light rum

30ml (1oz) brandy

15ml (½oz) gin

60ml (2oz) lemon juice

30ml (1oz) orange juice

sweet sherry

ice cubes

*Shake all the ingredients, except the
sherry, with ice. Pour into a hurricane
glass and float a layer of sherry
on top.*

Bloody Mary

MARGARITA

Margarita

45ml (1½ oz) premium tequila

30ml (1oz) Cointreau or triple sec

juice of half a lime and half a lemon

ice cubes

Garnish: lime wedge

Shake the ingredients with ice and serve in a salt-rimmed margarita glass on the rocks, or strain to serve 'up' in a chilled, salt-rimmed cocktail glass. Garnish with the lime wedge.

BLUE MARGARITA

45ml (1½ oz) tequila

22ml (¾ oz) blue curaçao

22ml (¾ oz) sour mix

ice cubes

Garnish: lime wedge

Shake all the ingredients with ice. Serve 'up', or on the rocks in a salt-rimmed glass and garnish with the lime wedge.

KIR

22ml (¾ oz) crème de cassis

white wine

Garnish: twist of lemon

Pour the crème de cassis in the
bottom of a wine glass or flute and
top up with wine. Garnish with a
twist of lemon.

ELECTRIC KOOL AID

15ml (½ oz) amaretto

15ml (½ oz) Midori

15ml (½ oz) cherry brandy

15ml (½ oz) triple sec

15ml (½ oz) Southern Comfort

15ml (½ oz) sour mix

15ml (½ oz) cranberry juice

1 dash grenadine

ice cubes

Shake the ingredients with ice. Strain
into a chilled cocktail glass or serve
over ice in a highball glass.

GOOM BAY SMASH

30ml (1oz) Myers's rum
or spiced rum

30ml (1oz) coconut rum

15ml (½ oz) crème de banane

1 splash orange juice

1 splash pineapple juice

ice cubes

Garnish: orange wheel and
maraschino cherry

Shake the ingredients with ice and
serve in hurricane or tall glass.
Garnish with a flag.

MAIDEN'S BLUSH COCKTAIL

22ml (¾ oz) absinthe
(or any substitute)

45ml (1½ oz) dry gin

1 tsp grenadine

ice cubes

Shake the ingredients with ice and
strain into a chilled cocktail glass.

WET WILLIE

30ml (1oz) vodka

30ml (1oz) amaretto

15ml (½ oz) triple sec

1 splash sour mix

lemon-lime soda (to fill)

ice cubes

Shake all the ingredients, except the
soda, with ice and strain over fresh
ice in a highball glass. Top up
with the soda.

GODFATHER

45ml (1½oz) Scotch

22ml (¾oz) amaretto

ice cubes

Build the ingredients over ice in a rocks glass.

WARD EIGHT

60ml (2oz) rye whiskey

1 splash fresh lime juice

1 splash fresh lemon juice

1 dash grenadine

ice cubes

Garnish: lemon wedge, orange wedge and maraschino cherry

Shake the ingredients with ice and strain into an ice-filled goblet. Garnish with the lemon and orange wedges, and the cherry.

VICTORIAN SECRET

60ml (2oz) Remy

30ml (1oz) Monin gingerbread syrup

15ml (½oz) fresh lemon juice

3 white raisins on a cocktail pick

ice cubes

Shake the Remy, Monin and lemon juice over ice for 15 seconds. Strain into a chilled martini glass. Spear the raisins with a cocktail pick, and rest it on top of the glass.
* Created by the Regans to be served alongside dessert at a dinner at the Bull and Bear in New York's Waldorf-Astoria hotel, 2003.

WALLIS BLUE

45ml (1½oz) gin

45ml (1½oz) triple sec

1 splash lime juice

ice cubes

Shake the ingredients with ice and strain into an ice-filled, sugar-frosted rocks glass.

AMARETTO SOUR

45ml (1½oz) amaretto

1 splash sour mix

ice cubes

Garnish: orange wheel and maraschino cherry

Shake the ingredients with ice and strain into a chilled cocktail glass. This drink can be served 'up' or on the rocks. Decorate with a flag.

COLLINS

37ml (1¼oz) spirit (of your choice)

½ tbsp powdered sugar

juice of half a lemon or a splash of sour mix

1 splash club soda

ice cubes

Garnish: orange wheel and maraschino cherry

Shake the liquor, sugar and sour mix with ice. Pour into a Collins glass and add the soda. Garnish with a flag.

Variations:

Tom Collins = gin
Vodka Collins = vodka
Rum Collins = rum
John Collins = whiskey
Irish Collins = Irish whiskey
Champagne Collins = substitute champagne for club soda, using the Tom Collins recipe.

Some say that the Tom Collins was named after 'Old Tom' Gin, which is a sweetened gin used rarely today. Most older recipes call for 'Old Tom'. There are also accounts that it was named after the creator of the drink. England, Australia and America have all laid claim. One American account puts this origin in the 19th century from an Irish immigrant, Tom Collins. He worked as a bartender in the New York garment area. It was intended as a thirst quencher to sip without 'getting tight'.

Here is his original recipe:

1 level tsp powdered sugar

juice of 1 lemon or 2 tbsp lemon juice

2 drops oil of orange

juice of half a lime

30ml (1oz) dry gin

soda water

Mix sugar, lemon juice and oil of orange in a tall water glass. Add lime juice and gin, stir well. Put in two medium lumps of ice, and fill to the top with soda water and stir.

RASPBERRY ICED TEA

15ml (½oz) gin

15ml (½oz) vodka

15ml (½oz) light rum

15ml (½oz) tequila

1 splash sour mix

1 splash cola

15ml (½oz) Chambord

ice cubes

Garnish: lemon wedge

Shake the ingredients with ice and strain into a chilled cocktail glass or over ice into a large tumbler or poco glass. Float Chambord on top. Garnish with the lemon wedge.

BAHAMA MAMA

45ml (1½oz) coconut rum

15ml (½oz) triple sec

1 splash cream of coconut

1 splash orange juice

1 splash pineapple juice

1 dash grenadine

ice cubes

Garnish: orange wheel and maraschino cherry

Shake the ingredients with ice and serve in a hurricane glass. Garnish with a flag.

BANSHEE

30ml (1oz) crème de banane

15ml (½oz) crème de cacao

1 splash half and half

ice cubes

Shake the ingredients with ice and strain into a champagne flute.

RASPBERRY CREAM

30ml (1oz) vodka

30ml (1oz) Chambord

1 splash half and half

ice cubes

Build over ice in a rocks glass.

GIRL SCOUT COOKIE

30ml (1oz) peppermint schnapps

15ml (½oz) Kahlúa

1 splash half and half

ice cubes

Stir the ingredients with ice and strain into a rocks glass.

WINDEX

Equal parts of vodka, triple sec, blue curaçao and sour mix

ice cubes

Build over ice in a highball glass.

TEQUILA SUNRISE

45ml (1½oz) tequila

orange juice (to fill)

1 dash grenadine

Pour the tequila and orange juice into a Collins glass over ice. Trickle grenadine on top.

FRENCH CONNECTION

37ml (1¼oz) cognac

22ml (¾oz) amaretto

ice cubes

Stir the ingredients with ice and strain into a brandy snifter or build over ice in an old-fashioned glass.

Tequila Sunrise

WOO WOO

30ml (1oz) peach schnapps

30ml (1oz) vodka

1 splash cranberry juice

ice cubes

Shake the ingredients with ice and strain into a chilled cocktail glass or over fresh ice in a highball glass.

POPPED CHERRY

60ml (2oz) vodka

15ml (½oz) raspberry schnapps

1 splash cranberry juice

1 splash club soda

ice cubes

Garnish: maraschino cherry

Build over ice in a highball glass. Slice the cherry halfway through and spear with a cocktail pick. Place the skewer on the rim of the glass.

ROB ROY

60ml (2oz) Scotch

15ml (½oz) sweet vermouth

1 dash bitters (if desired)

Garnish: maraschino cherry

Shake the ingredients with ice and strain into a chilled cocktail glass or build over ice in an old-fashioned glass. Garnish with the cherry.

Note: For a Perfect variation, use equal parts of sweet and dry vermouth and garnish with a twist of lemon. Use only dry vermouth for a dry version. Garnish with a twist of lemon.

Rob Roy

GINGERSNAP

30ml (1oz) ginger brandy

30ml (1oz) vodka

1 splash pineapple juice

2 splashes lemonade

ice cubes

Garnish: twist of lemon

Shake the ingredients with ice and pour into a tall or Collins glass. Garnish with the lemon twist.

FUZZY MELON

52ml (1¾oz) Midori

52ml (1¾oz) peach schnapps

30ml (1oz) blue curaçao

1 splash orange juice

1 splash pineapple juice

1 splash half and half

ice cubes

Shake the ingredients with ice and strain into a rocks glass.

ALTOID

Equal parts of Rumplemintz,
vodka, blue curaçao and
sour mix

ice cubes

*Shake the ingredients with ice and
strain into a chilled cocktail glass.*
* Created by Mike Saunders

MORNING GLORY

champagne (chilled)

orange juice

15ml (½oz) triple sec

Garnish: orange wheel

*Fill ¾ of a champagne saucer or
flute with the champagne. Add the
orange juice and triple sec. Garnish
with the orange wheel.*

CARIBBEAN BREEZE

60ml (2oz) coconut rum

30ml (1oz) vodka

1 splash orange juice

1 dash grenadine

ice cubes

Garnish: orange wheel and
maraschino cherry

*Build over ice in a Collins glass.
Decorate with a flag.*

CROCODILE COOLER

30ml (1oz) Absolut Citron

30ml (1oz) Midori

1 splash sour mix

lemon-lime soda (to fill)

ice cubes

*Shake together all the ingredients,
except the soda. Pour into a tall
glass over ice and top with soda.*

* I created the recipe below
for a Christmas party hosted
for teachers. The school's
morning announcements regu-
larly featured a weather fore-
cast; rain was known as …

LIQUID SUNSHINE

15ml (½oz) vodka

15ml (½oz) triple sec

15ml (½oz) crème de banane

15ml (½oz) white crème
de cacao

15ml (½oz) Galliano

1 splash orange juice

ice cubes

*Shake with ice and strain into a
Collins glass filled with ice.*

HIGHBALL

37ml (1¼oz) spirit of choice

1 splash water or soda

ice cubes

Build with your choice of spirit in a highball glass filled with ice.

X Y Z

30ml (1oz) rum

15ml (½oz) triple sec

1 splash sour mix

ice cubes

Shake the ingredients with ice and strain into a chilled cocktail glass.

BLOODY MARIA

dusting of pepper

1 dash Worcestershire sauce

1 dash lemon juice

2–3 drops Tabasco sauce

pinch of salt and celery salt

45ml (1½oz) tequila

tomato juice

ice cubes

Garnish: celery stick, lime wedge and jalapeño pepper (optional)

Build over ice in a tall glass. Start with the spices, add tequila, top up with tomato juice and stir. Garnish with the stick of celery, lime wedge and jalapeño pepper, if used.

STEPCHILD

45ml (1½oz) vodka

22ml (¾oz) amaretto

1 splash half and half

ice cubes

Build over ice in a highball glass or blend the ingredients with ice for a frozen drink.

MADRAS

37ml (1¼oz) vodka

1 splash cranberry juice

1 splash orange juice

ice cubes

Build over ice in a highball glass.

ITALIAN SURFER

30ml (1oz) amaretto

30ml (1oz) Malibu rum

1 splash cranberry

1 splash pineapple juice

ice cubes

Shake the ingredients with ice and strain over fresh ice in a highball glass.

ANTIFREEZE I

30ml (1oz) vodka

15ml (½oz) blue curaçao

15ml (½oz) crème de banane

ice cubes

1 splash orange juice

Garnish: maraschino cherry

Shake the ingredients with ice and serve in a highball glass. Garnish with the cherry.

SEX ON THE BEACH

30ml (1oz) vodka

22ml (¾oz) peach schnapps

22ml (¾oz) Chambord

1 splash pineapple juice

1 splash orange juice

1 splash cranberry juice

ice cubes

Shake the ingredients with ice and strain into an ice-filled Collins glass.

BELLINI

¼ part fresh peach purée, nectar or peach schnapps

¾ part champagne (chilled)

Garnish: peach slice (optional)

Pour the purée into a champagne flute. Top up with the champagne.

Bellini

SAZERAC

Pernod

37ml (1¼oz) whiskey or cognac

sugar to taste

3–4 dashes Peychaud's bitters

ice cubes (optional)

Garnish: twist or spiral of lemon

Swirl Pernod in a chilled old-fashioned glass to coat. Dissolve sugar in a few dashes of bitters to taste, add the ice and whiskey and shake. Strain into the prepared old-fashioned glass. Garnish with the lemon peel.

Sazerac

SMITH AND KERNS

37ml (1¼oz) Kahlúa

1 splash half and half

1 splash club soda

ice cubes

Shake the Kahlúa and half and half with ice and strain into an ice-filled highball glass. Add the splash of soda and serve.

DAY IN THE SHADE

30ml (1oz) Malibu rum

30ml (1oz) pineapple juice

15ml (½oz) cranberry juice

ice cubes

Shake the ingredients with ice and strain into a chilled cocktail glass or build on the rocks.

BLUE LAGOON

30ml (1oz) Malibu rum

15ml (½oz) blue curaçao

1 splash pineapple juice

ice cubes

Pour the rum and pineapple juice over ice in a highball or Collins glass. Float a layer of blue curaçao on top.

DYNASTY

45ml (1½oz) Southern Comfort

45ml (1½oz) amaretto

ice cubes

Shake the ingredients with ice. Strain into a chilled cocktail glass or build on the rocks.

BARN DOOR

45ml (1½oz) Scotch

30ml (1oz) triple sec

2 dashes orange bitters

ice cubes

Shake the ingredients with ice and strain into a rocks glass.

NUTS AND BERRIES

37ml (1¼oz) Chambord

37ml (1¼oz) Frangelico

1 splash half and half

ice cubes

Shake the ingredients with ice. Strain over fresh ice in a highball glass.

SOMBRERO

37ml (1¼oz) Kahlúa

1 splash half and half

ice cubes

Build over ice in a highball glass.

WHISKEY COCKTAIL

60ml (2oz) whiskey

1 tsp simple syrup

1 dash bitters

ice cubes

Garnish: maraschino cherry

Stir the ingredients over ice and strain into a chilled cocktail glass. Garnish with the cherry.

WIDOW WOODS NIGHTCAP

60ml (2oz) Scotch

15ml (½oz) dark crème de cacao

120ml (4oz) milk

ice cubes

Shake with ice and strain into a chilled cocktail glass.

HAWAIIAN COCKTAIL II

45ml (1½oz) Barbados rum

45ml (1½oz) pineapple juice

1 dash orange bitters

1 egg white

ice cubes

Shake the ingredients with ice and strain into a chilled cocktail glass.

UNION JACK COCKTAIL

45ml (1½ oz) gin

22ml (¾ oz) crème de yvette

1 dash grenadine

ice cubes

Shake the ingredients with ice and strain into a chilled cocktail glass.

BEE STINGER

45ml (1½ oz) blackberry brandy

15ml (½ oz) white crème de menthe

ice cubes

Shake the ingredients with ice and strain into a chilled cocktail glass.

SCREWDRIVER

37ml (1¼ oz) vodka

orange juice (to fill)

ice cubes

Build the ingredients over ice in a highball glass.

SEABREEZE

37ml (1¼ oz) vodka

1 splash grapefruit juice

1 splash cranberry juice

ice cubes

Build over ice in a highball glass.

DIRTY HARRY

30ml (1oz) Grand Marnier

30ml (1oz) Tia Maria

ice cubes

Stir the ingredients with ice and strain into a chilled cocktail glass or build on the rocks.

HIGH VOLTAGE

30ml (1oz) Scotch

22ml (¾ oz) Cointreau or triple sec

juice from half a lime or lemon

ice cubes

Shake the ingredients with ice and strain into a chilled cocktail glass.

SPRITZER

wine (of your choice)

club soda (to fill)

ice cubes

Garnish: twist of lemon

Fill a Collins glass with ice, pour half-full with wine, top up with the soda. Garnish with the twist of lemon.

LONG ISLAND ICED TEA

22ml (¾oz) rum

22ml (¾oz) gin

22ml (¾oz) vodka

22ml (¾oz) tequila

22ml (¾oz) triple sec

1 splash sour mix

1 splash cola

ice cubes

Shake the spirits and sour mix with ice. Pour into a hurricane, tall glass or tumbler. Add the cola. Garnish if you desire.

Long Island Iced Tea

FREDDY FUDDPUCKER

37ml (1¼oz) tequila

1 splash orange juice

Galliano

ice cubes

Pour the tequila and orange juice over ice in a rocks glass. Float a layer of Galliano on top.

SNOWSHOE

Equal parts of peppermint schnapps and brandy

ice cubes

Pour over ice in a snifter and serve.

DOWN UNDER

30ml (1oz) Irish whiskey

30ml (1oz) Bailey's Irish Cream

30ml (1oz) Kahlúa

1 splash half and half

ice cubes

Build over ice in a brandy snifter.

HURRICANE

45ml (1½oz) light rum
45ml (1½oz) dark rum
30ml (1oz) passion fruit syrup
22ml (¾oz) lime juice
ice cubes
Garnish: orange wheel and maraschino cherry

Shake the ingredients with ice and serve in a hurricane glass.
Garnish with a flag.

Pat O'Brien operated a speak-easy during Prohibition known as, 'Mr. O'Brien's Club Tipperary' in New Orleans. The password to get in was, 'storm's brewin''. In 1933, after the repeal of Prohibition, he moved across the street, opened Pat O'Briens, and later moved down to the present location at 718 St. Peter, in the French Quarter. During WWII, it was difficult to get whiskey, but rum was in ample supply. With the help of the liquor salesman, this cocktail was born. It is served in a 26oz hurricane glass, which is named after the shape of a hurricane lamp and the drink.

BLACK HAWK COCKTAIL

37ml (1¼oz) whiskey
37ml (1¼oz) sloe gin
ice cubes
Garnish: maraschino cherry

Shake the ingredients with ice and strain into a chilled cocktail glass.
Garnish with a cherry.

EYE OPENER

45ml (1½oz) light rum
15ml (½oz) triple sec
2 tsp Pernod
1 tsp crème de cacao
1 egg yolk
1 tsp sugar
ice cubes

Shake the ingredients with ice and strain into a chilled cocktail glass.

STINGER

| 45ml (1½ oz) brandy |
| 15ml (½ oz) white crème de menthe |
| ice cubes |

Shake the ingredients with ice and strain into a chilled cocktail glass or build over ice in a rocks glass.

APPLE JACK

| 15ml (½ oz) apple schnapps |
| 15ml (½ oz) bourbon |
| ice cubes |
| Garnish: cinnamon |

Build over ice in a rocks glass. Sprinkle the cinnamon on top.

BAY HORSE

| 45ml (1½ oz) whiskey |
| 15ml (½ oz) Pernod |
| 15ml (½ oz) dark crème de cacao |
| 30ml (1 oz) half and half |
| ice cubes |
| Garnish: nutmeg |

Shake the ingredients with ice and strain into an old-fashioned glass. Dust the nutmeg on top.

MIAMI SUNSET

| 30ml (1 oz) bourbon |
| 15ml (½ oz) triple sec |
| 1 splash orange juice |
| 1 dash grenadine |
| ice cubes |

Build the ingredients over ice in a highball glass.

BAILEY'S COMET II

| 30ml (1 oz) Bailey's Irish Cream |
| 30ml (1 oz) butterscotch schnapps |
| 30ml (1 oz) Goldschläger |
| 7ml (¼ oz) sambuca |
| ice cubes |
| Garnish: nutmeg |

Shake the first three liquors with ice and strain into a cocktail glass. Float a layer of sambuca on top and set alight. Sprinkle the nutmeg on top.

WARM FUZZY

Equal parts each of peach
schnapps and blue curaçao

ice cubes

Build over ice into a rocks glass.

BRANDY FIZZ

37ml (1¼oz) brandy

1 splash sour mix

1 dash club soda

ice cubes

Garnish: orange wheel
and maraschino cherry

*Shake the brandy and sour mix with
ice. Pour into a tall glass and top up
with the soda. Garnish with the
orange wheel and cherry.*

GIMLET

45ml (1½oz) gin or vodka

1 splash lime juice

ice cubes

Garnish: lime wedge

*Stir the ingredients with ice and
serve on the rocks in a rocks glass.
Alternatively, strain into a chilled
cocktail glass. Garnish with the
lime wedge.*

MOON BEAM

22ml (¾oz) amaretto

22ml (¾oz) white crème
de cacao

ice cubes

*Shake the ingredients with ice and
strain into a chilled cocktail glass.*

PEACH DELIGHT

15ml (½oz) peach schnapps

7ml (¼oz) vodka

7ml (¼oz) amaretto

1 splash cranberry juice

ice cubes

*Shake the ingredients with ice and
strain into a chilled cocktail glass.*

PINK LEMONADE

30ml (1oz) Absolut Citron or
Bacardi Limon

22ml (¾oz) triple sec

1 splash sour mix

1 splash cranberry juice

lemon-lime soda

ice cubes

*Shake the ingredients with ice and
strain into a chilled cocktail glass or
over ice in a highball glass.*

RAMOS GIN FIZZ

45ml (1½ oz) gin
45ml (1½ oz) half and half
15ml (½ oz) fresh lemon juice
15ml (½ oz) fresh lime juice
3 drops orange blossom water
1 tbsp powdered sugar
1 egg white
2 drops vanilla extract (optional)
club soda
cracked ice
Garnish: orange wheel

Put the ingredients in a blender with cracked ice, or shake vigorously in a cocktail shaker. Pour into a tall glass and add a squirt of club soda. Garnish with the orange wheel.

Henry C. Ramos came to New Orleans from Baton Rouge in 1888 to purchase the Imperial Cabinet Saloon. It was here that he began to make his mark with this cocktail that has been equated to 'drinking a flower'.

He bought the Stag Saloon in 1907, where the drink gained so much in popularity that people waited an hour sometimes to be served one. During the 1915 Mardi Gras, he employed 35 'shaker boys' and still could not keep up with the demand.

Ramos Gin Fizz

HORSE'S NECK

60ml (2oz) whiskey

1 lemon

1 splash ginger ale

ice cubes

Peel the rind of the lemon in one continuous strip. Place the spiral in a highball glass and drape one end of it over the rim of the glass. Fill with ice, add the whiskey and top with the ginger ale.

BANANA FANTASTIC

30ml (1oz) crème de banane

15ml (½oz) white crème de cacao

15ml (½oz) vodka

1 splash Galliano

1 splash half and half

ice cubes

Shake the ingredients with ice and strain into a goblet.

HAIRY NAVEL

37ml (1¼oz) vodka

22ml (¾oz) peach schnapps

1 splash orange juice

ice cubes

Build over ice in a highball glass.

MELON BALL

45ml (1½oz) Midori

30ml (1oz) vodka

1 splash orange juice

1 splash pineapple and/or grapefruit juice

ice cubes

Shake the ingredients with ice and strain into a chilled cocktail glass or serve over fresh ice in a highball glass.

ARNAUD'S SWAN COCKTAIL

60ml (2oz) Cognac

22ml (¾oz) Frangelico

15ml (½oz) fresh lemon juice

Garnish: maraschino cherry

Shake the ingredients together and strain into a champagne flute. Garnish with the cherry.

* Created by the Regans to accompany dessert at a Southern Comfort dinner at Arnauld's restaurant in New Orleans, September 18, 2003.

RUSSIAN BEAR

30ml (1oz) vodka

15ml (½oz) cream of coconut

1 splash half and half

ice cubes

Shake the ingredients with ice and strain into a chilled cocktail glass or over ice in a rocks glass.

POUSSE PLATTER

Equal parts each of Kahlúa, white crème de cacao, amaretto and half and half

ice cubes

Shake the ingredients with ice and strain into a chilled cocktail glass or over ice in a rocks glass.

GEORGIA PEACH

45ml (1½oz) peach schnapps

60ml (2oz) sour mix

15ml (½oz) grenadine

ice cubes

Garnish: lemon wheel and fresh peach slice

Shake with ice, strain over rocks in a highball glass. Garnish with the peach slice and lemon wheel.

BELMONT COCKTAIL

45ml (1½oz) gin

1 tsp raspberry syrup

22ml (¾oz) half and half

ice cubes

Shake the ingredients with ice and strain into a chilled cocktail glass.

ENGLISH HIGHBALL

22ml (¾oz) gin

22ml (¾oz) brandy

22ml (¾oz) sweet vermouth

1 splash ginger ale

ice cubes

Build over ice in a highball glass.

SPARKS

1 splash Absolut Peppar

champagne (chilled)

Pour the Peppar in a flute and top up with the champagne.

GREEN WITH ENVY

60ml (2oz) peach schnapps

30ml (1oz) blue curaçao

ice cubes

1 splash orange juice

1 slash apple juice

Build over ice in a Collins glass.

GOLDEN CADILLAC

30ml (1oz) Galliano

22ml (¾oz) white crème de cacao

22ml (¾oz) half and half or a scoop of vanilla ice cream

ice cubes

Shake the ingredients with ice and strain into a chilled cocktail glass or omit the ice and blend with ice cream for a frozen drink.

Golden Cadillac

KNOCK OUT COCKTAIL

22ml (¾oz) gin

dry vermouth

15ml (½oz) Pernod

1 tsp white crème de menthe

ice cubes

Garnish: maraschino cherry

Shake the ingredients with ice and strain into a chilled cocktail glass. Garnish with the cherry.

SHADY LADY

30ml (1oz) tequila

30ml (1oz) melon liqueur

120ml (4oz) grapefruit juice

ice cubes

Garnish: lime wedge and maraschino cherry

Build over ice in highball glass. Garnish with the lime wedge and cherry.

BLOODY BEER

1 splash tomato juice or
Bloody Mary mix

1 glass beer

*Pour the beer over tomato juice into
a chilled beer mug or pilsner.*

BOURBON AND BRANCH

37ml (1¼oz) bourbon

1 splash water

ice cubes

*Build the ingredients over ice in
a highball glass.*

TRINITY

Equal parts of peach
schnapps, apricot brandy
and Grand Marnier

ice cubes

*Build the ingredients over ice in
a rocks glass.*

SICILIAN KISS

45ml (1½oz) Southern Comfort

22ml (¾oz) amaretto

ice cubes

*Build the ingredients over ice in a
large rocks glass.*

BLUE MOTORCYCLE

15ml (½oz) gin

15ml (½oz) vodka

15ml (½oz) rum

15ml (½oz) blue curaçao

1 splash sour mix

1 splash lemon-lime soda

ice cubes

*Shake the ingredients with ice and
serve in a Collins glass. Top up with
the soda.*

BLOOD AND SAND

Equal parts of Scotch, cherry
brandy, sweet vermouth and
orange juice

ice cubes

*Shake the ingredients with ice and
strain into a chilled cocktail glass.*

ATTITUDE

30ml (1oz) vodka

30ml (1oz) amaretto

30ml (1oz) Malibu rum

1 splash cranberry

1 splash pineapple juice

ice cubes

*Shake the ingredients with ice. Strain
over fresh ice in a highball glass.*

OLD FASHIONED

1 splash simple syrup

1 dash bitters

60ml (2oz) whiskey or bourbon

1 splash club soda

Swirl the simple syrup and bitters around in a rocks glass to coat, add ice, pour in the liquor and top with the soda. Garnish with an orange wheel and cherry.

VARIATION

Muddle the orange wheel and cherry with simple syrup and bitters, making sure it coats most of the glass. Build the other ingredients as above.

ITALIAN SURFER WITH AN ATTITUDE

30ml (1oz) vodka

30ml (1oz) amaretto

30ml (1oz) Malibu rum

1 splash cranberry

1 splash pineapple juice

ice cubes

Shake the ingredients with ice. Strain over fresh ice in a highball glass.

MOJITO

mint leaves

1 dash simple syrup

1 dash bitters

1 splash lime juice

37ml (1¼oz) rum

crushed ice

club soda to fill (optional)

Muddle the mint leaves with the simple syrup and bitters in a highball glass. Add the ice, lime juice and rum. Top up with the soda, if used. Garnish with a sprig of fresh mint.

C-SPOT

37ml (1¼ oz) peach schnapps

1 splash cranberry juice

ice cubes

Garnish: orange wheel

Shake with ice and strain into a chilled cocktail glass. Garnish with the orange wheel.

BLOODHOUND

30ml (1oz) gin

15ml (½oz) sweet vermouth

15ml (½oz) dry vermouth

2 or 3 fresh strawberries

ice cubes

BLACK VELVET

Guinness Stout

champagne (chilled)

Pour the Guinness into a flute. Float a layer of champagne on top.

PINK LADY

45ml (1½ oz) gin

1 splash half and half

1 dash grenadine

ice cubes

Shake the ingredients with ice and strain into a champagne saucer or flute.

FAIR AND WARMER COCKTAIL

45ml (1½ oz) rum

22ml (¾ oz) sweet vermouth

1 dash orange curaçao

ice cubes

Stir the ingredients with ice and strain into a chilled cocktail glass.

Black Velvet

Crush the strawberries in a shaker, and add the ice and spirits. Shake the ingredients well and strain into a chilled cocktail glass.

GREYHOUND

37ml (1¼ oz) vodka

1 splash grapefruit juice

ice cubes

Build over ice in a highball glass.

MAI TAI

30ml (1oz) light rum

30ml (1oz) dark rum

15ml (½oz) orange curaçao

7ml (¼oz) simple syrup

7ml (¼oz) almond (orgeat) syrup

juice of 1 lime

ice cubes

Garnish: pineapple wedge, cherry and twist of lemon

Shake the ingredients with ice and serve in a cocktail glass. Garnish with the cherry, pineapple and twist of lemon.

FUZZY PIRATE

22ml (¾oz) peach schnapps

22ml (¾oz) Captain Morgan

1 dash orange curaçao

1 splash orange juice

ice cubes

Shake the ingredients with ice and strain into a chilled cocktail glass.

MILK PUNCH

30ml (1oz) whiskey

1 dash simple syrup

1 splash milk

ice cubes

Shake the ingredients with ice and strain into an ice-filled highball glass.

MEXICAN GRASSHOPPER

22ml (¾oz) Kahlúa

22ml (¾oz) white crème de cacao

22ml (¾oz) half and half

ice cubes

Shake the ingredients with ice and strain into a chilled cocktail glass or flute.

Mai Tai

PINEAPPLE UPSIDE DOWN CAKE

37ml (1¼oz) Licor 43 or vanilla vodka

1 splash pineapple juice

1 dash grenadine

ice cubes

Garnish: pineapple wedge and maraschino cherry

Shake the ingredients with ice and strain into a chilled cocktail glass. Garnish with the pineapple wedge and cherry.

Note: Vanilla vodka can be used if you prefer a less sweet drink.

FUZZY NAVEL

37ml (1¼oz) peach schnapps

1 splash orange juice

ice cubes

Build the ingredients over ice into a highball glass.

SOUTH PAW

Equal parts of brandy, orange juice and lemon-lime soda

ice cubes

Build the ingredients, in the order given, over ice in a highball glass.

LIBERTY COCKTAIL

45ml (1½oz) apple brandy

22ml (¾oz) rum

1 dash simple syrup

ice cubes

Shake with ice and strain into a chilled cocktail glass.

DIRTY MOTHER

37ml (1¼oz) brandy

22ml (¾oz) Kahlúa

1 splash half and half

ice cubes

Shake the ingredients with ice and serve in a rocks glass.

GREMLIN

45ml (1½oz) vodka

22ml (¾oz) blue curaçao

22ml (¾oz) rum

1 splash orange juice

ice cubes

Shake the ingredients with ice and strain into a chilled cocktail glass.

SAVOY COCKTAIL

Equal parts of crème de cacao,
Benedictine and brandy

Layer in a pony or Pousse Café glass.

BMW

Equal parts of Bailey's, Malibu
and white crème de cacao

ice cubes

*Shake the ingredients with ice and
strain into a chilled cocktail glass;
alternatively, serve on the rocks.*

ROOT BEER FLOAT

30ml (1oz) vodka

22ml (¾oz) Galliano

1 splash half and half

1 splash cola

ice cubes

*Shake the ingredients with ice and
strain over ice in a highball glass.*

FUDGESICLE

30ml (1oz) vodka

7ml (¼oz) dark crème
de cacao

7ml (¼oz) chocolate syrup

*Shake the ingredients with ice and
serve in a rocks glass.*

SCORPION

30ml (1oz) brandy

30ml (1oz) rum

90ml (3oz) pineapple juice

1 dash grenadine

ice cubes

*Shake the ingredients with ice and
strain into an ice-filled highball glass.*

JAMAICA HOP

30ml (1oz) Kahlúa

30ml (1oz) white crème
de cacao

30ml (1oz) half and half

ice cubes

*Shake the ingredients with ice and
strain into a chilled cocktail glass.*

MONKEY GLAND

45ml (1½oz) gin

30ml (1oz) orange juice

2 dashes grenadine

2 dashes Benedictine

ice cubes

*Shake the ingredients with ice and
strain into a chilled cocktail glass.*

PEARL HARBOUR

Equal parts of vodka, Midori and pineapple juice

ice cubes

Shake the ingredients with ice and strain into a chilled cocktail glass.

BOMBINO

37ml (1¼oz) vodka

22ml (¾oz) amaretto

1 splash half and half

ice cubes

Shake the ingredients together with ice and serve over ice in a rocks glass.

ORANGE BLOSSOM

37ml (1¼oz) gin

1 splash orange juice

ice cubes

Build over ice in a highball glass.

HOLLYWOOD

45ml (1½oz) vodka

22ml (¾oz) Chambord

1 splash pineapple juice

ice cubes

Stir the ingredients over ice and strain into a snifter.

COLORADO MOTHER

Equal parts of Kahlúa, vodka, gin, rum, tequila and half and half

1 splash cola

ice cubes

Shake all the ingredients, except the cola, with ice. Pour into a tall glass and top up with the cola.

FUZZY PEACH

30ml (1oz) vodka

30ml (1oz) peach schnapps

1 splash grapefruit juice

1 dash grenadine

ice cubes

Build the ingredients over ice, in the order given, in a highball glass.

MARTINIS

There are many recipes in this section that are really not considered martinis, according to the 'old school'. Many still insist that a martini is only made with gin and vermouth. But today a martini can be made with any white liquor, and its preparation often varies according to the consumer's preference. Some prefer their martinis served on the rocks or straight up with the ice cubes in a seperate glass, while others prefer it with olives, or without. It's all a matter of choice!

Before we get started with the recipes, let's take a look at the the first martini.

There are many stories about who actually invented the first martini, including the eminent mixologist Professor Jerry Thomas. However JP Schwartzendorf, an 18th-century German opera composer, was nicknamed 'Martini', and seems to have invented the first martini. He used the original gin, genièvre, from Belgium.

His recipe calls for:
30ml (2oz) genièvre
30ml (1oz) Chablis or Rhine wine
1/16 tsp cinnamon

The martini somehow evolved into American culture and from there it became the drink of choice for decades. Robert Agneau, a bartender in New York, is credited as being the first to add the olive. It was to make the gin taste a bit more palatable.

THE ORIGINAL AMERICAN MARTINI RECIPE

45ml (1½oz) gin
15ml (½oz) sweet vermouth
15ml (½oz) dry vermouth
1 dash orange bitters
ice cubes

Stir the ingredients with ice and strain into a chilled cocktail glass.

THE CLASSIC MARTINI

45ml (1½oz) gin
15ml (½oz) dry vermouth
ice cubes

Stir the ingredients with ice and strain into a chilled cocktail glass.

GOLDEN MARTINI

60ml (2oz) golden gin
15ml (½oz) dry vermouth
Garnish: olives

Stir the ingredients with ice and strain into a chilled cocktail glass. Alternatively, serve on the rocks. Garnish with a spear of olives.

THE MODERN MARTINI

45ml (1½oz) gin or vodka

7ml (¼oz) dry vermouth

ice cubes

Stir or shake the ingredients with ice and strain into a chilled cocktail glass.

VARIATIONS

Dry – Less or no vermouth; serve with a twist of lemon.
Sweet – Substitute sweet for the dry vermouth.
Gibson – Serve with three cocktail onions.

Dirty – Add one splash of olive juice.
Filthy – Omit the vermouth and add more olive juice.
Cajun – Garnish wih a jalapeño pepper.

SILK PANTY

30ml (1oz) peach schnapps

30ml (1oz) vodka

30ml (1oz) cranberry juice

ice cubes

Stir the ingredients with ice and strain into a chilled cocktail glass.

There are many variations to the martini (from left to right: Dry, Medium and Sweet Martini).

ALOHA

30ml (1oz) gin

30ml (1oz) triple sec

1 dash pineapple juice

ice cubes

Shake the ingredients with ice and strain into a chilled cocktail glass.

SLY FOX

45ml (1½oz) gin

1 splash Grand Marnier

ice cubes

Shake or stir the ingredients with ice and serve on the rocks. Alternatively, strain into a chilled cocktail glass.

FIFTY FIFTY COCKTAIL

45ml (1½oz) gin

45ml (1½oz) dry vermouth

ice cubes

Stir the ingredients with ice and strain into a chilled cocktail glass.

FLIRTINI

fresh raspberries

15ml (½oz) Stolichnaya Razberi vodka

15ml (½oz) Cointreau

1 splash lime juice

1 splash pineapple juice

1 splash cranberry juice

brut champagne (to fill)

Garnish: sprig of mint

Muddle a few raspberries in the bottom of a cocktail glass. Shake the other five ingredients together and strain into a chilled cocktail glass. Top up with the champagne and garnish with the sprig of mint.

THE PERFECT MARTINI

30ml (1oz) gin

30ml (1oz) dry vermouth

30ml (1oz) sweet vermouth

ice cubes

Stir the ingredients with ice and strain into a chilled cocktail glass.

VARIATIONS

Cooperstown – Garnish with a sprig of mint.

Cardinale – Add a dash of Campari.

Turf Cocktail – Add a dash of bitters and absinthe.

Lone Tree – Garnish with an orange peel.

BLUE SKY MARTINI

15ml (½ oz) Skyy vodka

7ml (¼ oz) blue curaçao

ice cubes

Garnish: twist of lemon

Shake the ingredients with ice and serve on the rocks. Alternatively, strain into a chilled cocktail glass. Garnish with the twist of lemon.

ADMIRAL BENBOW

60ml (2oz) gin

30ml (1oz) dry vermouth

ice cubes

Garnish: maraschino cherry

Stir the ingredients with ice and strain into a chilled cocktail glass. Garnish with the cherry.

RASPBERTINI

45ml (1½ oz) raspberry vodka

22ml (¾ oz) Chambord

15ml (½ oz) white crème de cacao

ice cubes

Shake the ingredients with ice and strain into a chilled cocktail glass.

GIN COCKTAIL

60ml (2oz) gin

2 dashes orange bitters

ice cubes

Garnish: twist of lemon

Stir the ingredients with ice and strain into a chilled cocktail glass. Garnish with the twist of lemon.

CORKSCREW

45ml (1½ oz) rum

15ml (½ oz) dry vermouth

15ml (½ oz) peach brandy

ice cubes

Garnish: lime wedge

Stir the ingredients with ice and strain into a chilled cocktail glass. Garnish with the lime wedge.

ZAZA

45ml (1½ oz) gin

22ml (¾ oz) Dubonnet

ice cubes

Garnish: twist of orange

Stir the ingredients with ice and strain into a chilled cocktail glass. Garnish with the twist of orange.

BLACK MARTINI

60ml (2oz) vodka
30ml (1oz) Chambord
15ml (½oz) blue curaçao
ice cubes

Shake the ingredients with ice and strain into a chilled cocktail glass.

MARTINI ROYALE

90ml (3oz) vodka or gin (chilled)
champagne (chilled) to fill
Garnish: twist of lemon

Pour the vodka or gin in a chilled cocktail glass. Top up with the champagne and garnish with the twist of lemon.

Cosmopolitan

COSMOPOLITAN

45ml (1½oz) Absolut Citron
22ml (¾oz) Cointreau or triple sec
1 dash lime juice
1 dash cranberry juice
ice cubes
Garnish: twist of lemon or lime wheel

Shake the ingredients with ice and strain into a chilled cocktail glass. Garnish with a lemon or lime wheel.

VESPER

60ml (2oz) gin
30ml (1oz) vodka
1 splash Lillet
ice cubes
Garnish: twist of lemon

Shake the ingredients with ice and serve on the rocks. Alternatively, strain and serve 'up' in a chilled cocktail glass. Garnish with the twist of lemon.

SAKÉTINI

Sakétini

37ml (1¼oz) gin

1 splash saké

ice cubes

Garnish: olive

Stir the ingredients with ice and strain into a chilled cocktail glass.

Serve this drink garnished with the olive.

BRANTINI

15ml (½ oz) brandy

30ml (1oz) gin

1 splash dry vermouth

ice cubes

Garnish: twist of lemon

Shake the ingredients with ice and serve on the rocks. Alternatively, strain into a chilled cocktail glass. Garnish with the twist of lemon.

ORANGE DROP

45ml (1½ oz) orange vodka

22ml (¾ oz) Cointreau

15ml (½ oz) orange curaçao

ice cubes

Garnish: orange wheel

Stir the ingredients with ice and strain into a chilled cocktail glass. Garnish with the orange wheel.

HENNESSY MARTINI

52ml (1¾ oz) Hennessy

1 splash lemon juice

ice cubes

Garnish: twist of lemon

Shake the ingredients with ice and strain into a chilled cocktail glass. Garnish with the twist of lemon.

BLUE MARTINI

45ml (1½ oz) gin

15ml (½ oz) dry vermouth

15ml (½ oz) blue curaçao

ice cubes

Garnish: twist of lime

Shake the ingredients with ice and strain into a chilled cocktail glass. Garnish with the twist of lime.

VESUVIO

30ml (1oz) light rum

15ml (½ oz) sweet vermouth

ice cubes

Shake the ingredients with ice and serve on the rocks. Alternatively, strain into a chilled cocktail glass.

WASHINGTON COCKTAIL

45ml (1½ oz) dry vermouth

22ml (¾ oz) brandy

2 dashes bitters

1 dash simple syrup

ice cubes

Stir the ingredients with ice and strain into a chilled cocktail glass.

HASTY COCKTAIL

45ml (1½ oz) gin

22ml (¾ oz) dry vermouth

1 dash grenadine

1 drop Pernod

ice cubes

Stir the ingredients with ice and strain into a chilled cocktail glass.

SILVER BULLET

45ml (1½ oz) gin

1 splash Scotch

ice cubes

Shake or stir the ingredients with ice and serve on the rocks, or strain into a chilled cocktail glass.

WALLICK COCKTAIL

37ml (1¼ oz) gin

37ml (1¼ oz) dry vermouth

1 tsp orange curaçao

ice cubes

Stir the ingredients with ice and strain into a chilled cocktail glass.

BEADLESTONE COCKTAIL

45ml (1½ oz) Scotch

45ml (1½ oz) dry vermouth

ice cubes

Stir the ingredients with ice and strain into a chilled cocktail glass.

NEGRONI

22ml (¾ oz) Campari

22ml (¾ oz) gin

22ml (¾ oz) sweet vermouth

ice cubes

Stir the ingredients with ice and strain into a chilled cocktail glass.

CARUSO

45ml (1½ oz) gin

30ml (1oz) dry vermouth

1 splash green crème de menthe

ice cubes

Stir the ingredients with ice and strain into a chilled cocktail glass.

GOLDFINGER

60ml (2oz) vodka

30ml (1oz) Goldschläger

ice cubes

Stir the ingredients with ice and strain into a chilled cocktail glass.

CHOCOLATE MARTINI

Chocolate Martini (left) and Tequini

45ml (1½oz) chocolate vodka

30ml (1oz) white crème
de cacao

ice cubes

Garnish: cocoa powder and
grated chocolate

*Shake the ingredients with ice and
strain into a chilled cocktail glass
that has been rimmed with cocoa
powder. Garnish with the grated
chocolate.*

Note: *Pour slowly to avoid getting
the cocoa powder from the rim of
the glass into the drink. If you are*
*really crafty, rim the chilled glass
with chocolate sauce and place the
glass into the freezer until you are
ready to serve the drink.*

TEQUINI

45ml (1½oz) tequila

1 splash dry vermouth

ice cubes

*Shake the ingredients with ice and
serve on the rocks. Alternatively,
strain into a chilled cocktail glass.*

Bronx Cocktail

FLYING DUTCHMAN

60ml (2oz) gin

1 dash triple sec

ice cubes

Shake the ingredients with ice and strain into a chilled cocktail glass.

SILVER BULLET COCKTAIL

45ml (1½oz) peppermint schnapps

22ml (¾oz) vodka

ice cubes

Shake or stir the ingredients with ice and serve on the rocks, or strain into a chilled cocktail glass.

BRONX COCKTAIL

30ml (1oz) gin

15ml (½oz) dry vermouth

15ml (½oz) sweet vermouth

1 splash orange juice

ice cubes

Garnish: orange wheel (optional)

Shake the ingredients with ice. Strain into a chilled cocktail glass and garnish with the orange wheel, if used.

DIRTY MARTINI

45ml (1½oz) gin or vodka

7ml (¼oz) dry vermouth (optional)

1 splash olive juice

ice cubes

Stir the ingredients with ice and strain into a chilled cocktail glass.

BLUE FIN

60ml (2oz) Hpnotiq

30ml (1oz) Absolut Citron

1 splash white cranberry juice

ice cubes

Shake the ingredients with ice and strain into a chilled cocktail glass.

BLACK DEVIL COCKTAIL

60ml (2oz) rum

15ml (½oz) dry vermouth

ice cubes

Garnish: black olive

Shake the ingredients with ice and strain into a chilled cocktail glass. Garnish with the black olive.

GYPSY COCKTAIL

37ml (1¼oz) gin

37ml (¼oz) sweet vermouth

ice cubes

Garnish: maraschino cherry

Stir the ingredients with ice and strain into a chilled cocktail glass. Garnish with the cherry.

PARISIAN

60ml (2oz) gin

30ml (1oz) dry vermouth

15ml (½oz) crème de cassis

ice cubes

Stir the ingredients with ice and strain into a chilled cocktail glass.

GIBSON

60ml (2oz) gin or vodka

1 dash dry vermouth

ice cubes

Garnish: cocktail onions

Stir the ingredients with ice and strain into a chilled cocktail glass. Garnish with skewered cocktail onions.

MISTICO MARTINI

30ml (1oz) Jose Cuervo Mistico

30ml (1oz) Chambord

30ml (1oz) sour mix

ice cubes

Stir the ingredients with ice and strain into a chilled cocktail glass. Serve ungarnished.

APÉRITIFS

An apéritif is a drink served before a meal to whet the appetite. The term, derived from the Latin word *aperire,* is French and it means 'to open'. Although most cocktails can be classified as apéritifs, as long as they are not sweet, the most traditional ones contain bitters, wine-based spirits such as vermouth, quinine-flavoured spirits or beer. So, even though a Bloody Mary or a Margarita may be a perfect apéritif for you, these recipes will not appear in this section but rather in the cocktails recipe section.

ALGONQUIN

45ml (1½oz) whiskey

30ml (1oz) dry vermouth

30ml (1oz) pineapple juice

ice cubes

Shake the ingredients with ice and strain into a chilled cocktail glass.

KEY LARGO

22ml (¾oz) Campari

7ml (¼oz) triple sec

1 splash grapefruit juice

1 splash club soda

Build the Campari, triple sec and grapefruit juice in a highball glass. Finish with the splash of soda.

DELMONICO

37ml (¼oz) gin

15ml (½oz) brandy

15ml (½oz) sweet vermouth

15ml (½oz) dry vermouth

2 dashes bitters

ice cubes

Garnish: twist of lemon

Shake the ingredients with ice and strain into a chilled cocktail glass. Garnish with the twist of lemon.

DUBONNET COCKTAIL

37ml (1¼oz) Dubonnet

37ml (1¼oz) gin

1 dash bitters

ice cubes

Garnish: twist of lemon

Build the ingredients over ice in a rocks glass. Garnish with the twist of lemon.

AFFINITY COCKTAIL

30ml (1oz) Scotch

30ml (1oz) sweet vermouth

30ml (1oz) dry vermouth

3 dashes orange bitters

ice cubes

Stir the ingredients with ice. Strain the mixture into a chilled cocktail glass.

WILL ROGERS

45ml (1½oz) gin

15ml (½oz) dry vermouth

1 dash triple sec

1 splash orange juice

ice cubes

Shake the ingredients with ice and strain into a chilled cocktail glass.

LUXURY COCKTAIL

90ml (3oz) brandy

90ml (3oz) champagne (chilled)

2 dashes orange bitters

Stir the ingredients together gently,
pour into a large champagne saucer
and serve.

AMERICANO HIGHBALL

30ml (1oz) Campari

60ml (2oz) sweet vermouth

1 splash club soda

ice cubes

Garnish: twist of lemon

Pour the Campari and vermouth over
ice in a highball glass. Top up with
the soda and garnish with the twist
of lemon.

WHIP COCKTAIL

45ml (1½oz) brandy

15ml (½oz) sweet vermouth

15ml (½oz) dry vermouth

1 tsp triple sec

¼ tsp anisette

ice cubes

Stir the ingredients with ice and
strain into a chilled cocktail glass.

YASHMAK

22ml (¾oz) whiskey

22ml (¾oz) dry vermouth

1 splash Campari

ice cubes

Shake the ingredients with ice and
strain into a Collins glass filled with
fresh ice cubes.

BIJOU COCKTAIL

22ml (¾oz) green Chartreuse

22ml (¾oz) gin

22ml (¾oz) sweet vermouth

1 dash orange bitters

ice cubes

Garnish: maraschino cherry

Shake the ingredients with ice and
strain into a chilled cocktail glass.
Garnish with the cherry.

VELL AMIC

30ml (1oz) Dubonnet

30ml (1oz) Grand Marnier

30ml (1oz) gin

ice cubes

Garnish: maraschino cherry

Stir the ingredients with ice and
strain into a chilled cocktail glass.
Garnish with the cherry.

LITTLE PRINCESS
COCKTAIL

Little Princess Cocktail

37ml (1¼oz) light rum

37ml (1¼oz) sweet vermouth

ice cubes

*Stir the ingredients with ice and
strain into a chilled cocktail glass.*

MADURO COCKTAIL

Equal parts of Punt è Mes and sweet vermouth (for a drier cocktail, use dry vermouth)

ice cubes

orange peel

Stir the Punt è Mes and vermouth with ice, and strain into a chilled cocktail glass. Ignite the orange peel by holding it skin-side down about 5cm (2in) over the drink and passing it through the flame so that the oils flare up and drop onto the surface of the drink.
*Created by Dale DeGroff –
(kingcocktail.com)

VICTOR

45ml (1½oz) gin

15ml (½oz) sweet vermouth

15ml (½oz) brandy

ice cubes

Shake the ingredients with ice and strain into a chilled cocktail glass.

DUCHESS COCKTAIL

22ml (¾oz) Pernod

22ml (¾oz) sweet vermouth

22ml (¾oz) dry vermouth

ice cubes

Stir the ingredients with ice and strain into a chilled cocktail glass.

MERRY WIDOW

45ml (1½oz) gin

45ml (1½oz) sweet vermouth

1 dash Pernod

1 dash bitters

ice cubes

Garnish: twist of lemon

Build the ingredients over ice in a rocks glass. Alternatively, shake the ingredients with ice and strain into a chilled cocktail glass. Garnish with the twist of lemon.

Merry Widow

EL PRESIDENTE

15ml (½oz) French vermouth

30ml (1oz) light rum

1 tsp grenadine

1 dash orange curaçao

ice cubes

Stir the ingredients with ice and strain into a chilled cocktail glass.

BENTLEY

30ml (1oz) Dubonnet

45ml (1½oz) apple brandy

ice cubes

Garnish: twist of lemon

Shake the ingredients with ice and strain into a chilled cocktail glass. Serve garnished with the twist of lemon.

BITTERS HIGHBALL

22ml (¾oz) bitters

club soda or ginger ale (to fill)

Garnish: twist of lemon

Pour the bitters into a highball glass and top up with the soda or ginger ale. Garnish with the twist of lemon.

ADONIS

22ml (¾oz) sweet vermouth

45ml (1½oz) dry sherry

1 dash orange bitters

ice cubes

Stir the ingredients with ice and strain into a chilled cocktail glass.

WEBSTER COCKTAIL

30ml (1oz) gin

15ml (½oz) dry vermouth

15ml (½oz) apricot brandy

1 splash lime juice

ice cubes

Shake the ingredients with ice, strain into a chilled cocktail glass and serve.

GIN AND BITTERS (PINK GIN)

bitters

75ml (2½oz) gin (chilled)

Pour the bitters into a cocktail glass. Swirl the glass until the inside is entirely coated with the bitters – shake out the excess. Fill the glass with the gin.

MANHATTAN

45ml (1½oz) whiskey or bourbon

22ml (¾oz) sweet vermouth

1 dash bitters (if desired)

Garnish: maraschino cherry

Build the ingredients in a rocks glass, or stir with ice and strain into a chilled cocktail glass. Garnish with the cherry.

VARIATION

Perfect Manhattan – Use equal parts of sweet and dry vermouth. Garnish with a twist of lemon.

EAST INDIA II

37ml (1¼oz) dry vermouth

37ml (1¼oz) sherry

1 dash bitters

ice cubes

Stir the ingredients with ice and strain into a chilled cocktail glass.

XERES

60ml (2oz) dry sherry

1 dash bitters

ice cubes

Stir the ingredients with ice and strain into a chilled cocktail glass.

ITALIAN ICED TEA

37ml (1¼oz) sweet vermouth

37ml (1¼oz) ginger ale

ice cubes

Garnish: twist of lemon

Build the ingredients over ice in a Collins glass. Garnish with the twist of lemon.

FRENCH KISS

30ml (1oz) dry vermouth

30ml (1oz) sweet vermouth

ice cubes

Garnish: lime wedge

Build the ingredients over ice in an old-fashioned glass. Garnish with the lime wedge.

BERMUDA HIGHBALL

22ml (¾oz) gin

22ml (¾oz) brandy

22ml (¾oz) dry vermouth

1 splash ginger ale or club soda

Garnish: twist of lemon

Build the ingredients in a highball glass. Serve garnished with the twist of lemon.

WESTERN ROSE

30ml (1oz) gin

15ml (½oz) apricot brandy

15ml (½oz) dry vermouth

¼ tsp lemon juice

ice cubes

Shake the ingredients with ice and strain into a chilled cocktail glass.

VERMOUTH CASSIS

45ml (1½oz) dry vermouth

22ml (¾oz) crème de cassis

1 splash club soda

ice cubes

Stir the vermouth and crème de cassis with ice in a highball glass. Add the soda and stir all the ingredients together.

WOODWARD COCKTAIL

45ml (1½oz) Scotch

15ml (½oz) dry vermouth

1 tbsp grapefruit juice

ice cubes

Shake the ingredients with ice. Strain into a chilled cocktail glass and serve ungarnished.

WEEP NO MORE

45ml (1½oz) Dubonnet

45ml (1½oz) cognac

1 splash lime juice

1 dash cherry liqueur

ice cubes

Shake the ingredients with ice, strain into a chilled cocktail glass and serve.

YALE COCKTAIL

45ml (1½oz) gin

15ml (½oz) dry vermouth

1 tsp crème de yvette or blue curaçao

1 dash bitters

ice cubes

Stir the ingredients with ice, strain into a chilled cocktail glass and serve.

SHOOTERS

Most shooters get their names from their flavours, colours or resemblance, while others simply have risqué names. Many shooters have become popular just by the way they are imbibed. Shooters are a fun and versatile way to get a party started. They often accompany another drink, like beer. It is wise to watch your or others' consumption of shooters because they are potent little drinks and as much fun as they are, they can and will sneak up on you!

A good idea is to not mix too many shooters. If you are drinking more than one, rather stick to the same kind or combine only those that contain basically the same types of spirits.

There are many occasions that call for shooters, most commonly in celebration. In this case, everyone generally raises and clinks glasses to a toast.

Here are a few translations of the basic toast:
English – Cheers!
Chinese – Wen Lie!
French – A votre santé!
German – Prosit!
Greek – Yasas!
Hebrew – L'Chayim!
Hungarian – Ege'sze'ge're!
Irish – Slainte!
Italian – Alla Salute!
Japanese – Kanpai!
Polish – Na Zdrowie!
Russian – Za vashe zdorovye!
Spanish – Salud!
Swedish – Skal!

DIAMOND JIM

30ml (1oz) rum

15ml (½oz) amaretto

1 splash orange juice

1 splash cranberry juice

1 splash pineapple juice

1 splash sour mix

ice cubes

Shake the ingredients with ice and strain into a chilled cocktail, pony or rocks glass.

RATTLESNAKE

2 parts Kahlúa

3 parts amaretto

1 part half and half

Layer the ingredients, in the order given, in a pony or shot glass. Alternatively, strain into a chilled cocktail or rocks glass.

KEOKI SHOOTER

15ml (½oz) hot coffee

15ml (½oz) Kahlúa

15ml (½oz) dark crème de cacao

7ml (¼oz) brandy

whipped cream

Build in a cordial glass and top with the whipped cream.

DEATH WISH

Equal parts of grenadine, Wild Turkey liqueur, peppermint schnapps and 151 rum

Layer the ingredients, in the order given, in a pony or shot glass.

ALLIGATOR

Equal parts of Midori, Malibu and pineapple juice

1 dash Chambord

Jägermeister

ice cubes

Shake the Midori, Malibu and pineapple juice with ice and strain into a chilled cocktail glass. Drop in the dash of Chambord and let it fall to the bottom of the glass. Float a thin layer of Jägermeister on top.

MIND ERASER

Equal parts of Kahlúa and vodka

1 splash club soda

ice cubes

In a rocks glass filled with ice, add the ingredients in the order given. Drink through a straw.

Z STREET SLAMMER

37ml (1¼oz) Myers's rum

22ml (¾oz) crème de banane and pineapple juice

7ml (¼oz) grenadine

ice cubes

Shake the ingredients with ice and strain into a chilled cocktail, pony or rocks glass.

TOMAKAZI

37ml (1¼oz) gin

1 splash lime juice

1 splash sour mix

ice cubes

Shake the ingredients with ice and strain into a chilled cocktail, pony or rocks glass.

STORM CLOUD

30ml (1oz) amaretto or coffee liqueur

15ml (½oz) 151 rum

2 drops half and half

ice cubes

Stir the liqueurs and rum with ice and strain into a chilled cocktail or rocks glass. Drop the cream into the shot using a hollow swizzle stick.

PURPLE HOOTER

Equal parts of vodka,
Chambord and sour mix

1 splash 7-Up

Shake the ingredients with ice and strain into a chilled cocktail, pony or rocks glass. Top up with the 7-Up.

BANANA BOOMER

15ml (½oz) vodka

15ml (½oz) crème de banane

ice cubes

Stir or shake the ingredients with ice and strain into a chilled cocktail, pony or rocks glass.

RED HOT

30ml (1oz) cinnamon schnapps

2 or 3 drops Tabasco sauce

Stir the ingredients in a shot glass.

SANTA CLAUS IS COMING TO TOWN

Equal parts of Rumplemintze, cinnamon schnapps, Midori and whipped cream

Mix the ingredients and serve in a chilled champagne saucer. Top with whipped cream.

BLUE MOON

Equal parts of blue curaçao, amaretto and Bailey's Irish Cream

Layer the ingredients, in the order given, in a pony or shot glass.

KANDY KANE

22ml (¾oz) Rumplemintze

7ml (¼oz) crème de noyaux

Layer the ingredients, in the order given, in a pony or shot glass.

MISDEMEANOUR

Equal parts of Crown Royal and butterscotch schnapps

ice cubes

Shake the ingredients with ice and strain into a chilled cocktail, pony or rocks glass. (Any more than a few and it is a felony.)

GREEN APPLE

30ml (1oz) apple schnapps

1 dash lime juice

Stir the ingredients with ice and strain into a salt-rimmed, chilled cocktail or rocks glass.

SIMPLY BONKERS

Equal parts of Chambord, rum
and half and half

ice cubes

*Shake the ingredients with ice and
strain into a chilled cocktail, pony
or rocks glass.*

THUMB SUCKER

Equal parts of white crème de
menthe, Bailey's Irish Cream
and Kahlúa

ice cubes

*Shake the ingredients with ice and
strain into a chilled cocktail, pony
or rocks glass.*

BUBBLE GUM

15ml (½oz) vodka

15ml (½oz) Midori

15ml (½oz) crème de banane

15ml (½oz) orange juice

15ml (½oz) sour mix

7ml (¼oz) grenadine

ice cubes

*Shake the ingredients with ice and
strain into a chilled cocktail, pony
or rocks glass.*

BUSTED NUMBER

Equal parts of raspberry
schnapps, Bailey's Irish
Cream and Grand Marnier

*Layer the ingredients, in the order
given, in a pony or shot glass.*

ROCK LOBSTER II

Equal parts of white crème de
cacao, amaretto, Bailey's Irish
Cream and half and half

Garnish: cinnamon

*Layer the ingredients, in the order
given, in a shot or pony glass.
Sprinkle a dusting of cinnamon
on top.*

SCREAMING O

Equal parts of Bailey's Irish
Cream, Kahlúa and amaretto

vodka

ice cubes

*Stir the Bailey's, Kahlúa and
amaretto with ice and strain into a
rocks glass or large shot glass. Layer
the vodka on top.*

ORGASM

22ml (¾oz) amaretto

22ml (¾oz) Kahlúa

22ml (¾oz) Bailey's Irish Cream

ice cubes

Shake the ingredients with ice and strain into a shot glass.

Screaming O

FUNKY MONKEY

Equal parts of peach schnapps, Kahlúa and Bailey's Irish Cream

ice cubes

Shake the schnapps and Kahlúa with ice and strain into a chilled cocktail, pony or rocks glass. Float a layer of Bailey's Irish Cream on top.

DRINK DON'T LIE

15ml (½oz) sambuca

15ml (½oz) tequila

3 dashes Tabasco sauce

Layer the tequila on top of the sambuca in a shot glass. Add the Tabasco, which should form a red layer between the two spirits.

LEG STRETCHER

15ml (½oz) Malibu

15ml (½oz) vodka

15ml (½oz) Midori

1 splash pineapple juice

1 splash lemon-lime soda

ice cubes

Shake the Malibu, vodka, Midori and pineapple juice with ice and strain into a chilled cocktail, pony or rocks glass. Top up with the soda.

SEPARATOR

Equal parts of blackberry
brandy, Kahlúa and half
and half

ice cubes

*Shake the ingredients with ice and
strain into a chilled cocktail, pony
or rocks glass.*

PANAMA RED

37ml (1¼ oz) Jose Cuervo

22ml (¾ oz) triple sec

1 dash sour mix

1 dash grenadine

ice cubes

*Shake the ingredients with ice and
strain into a chilled cocktail, pony
or rocks glass.*

SKITTLE

15ml (½ oz) vodka

15ml (½ oz) cranberry juice

15ml (½ oz) sour mix

7ml (¼ oz) crème de banane

1 dash grenadine

ice cubes

*Shake the ingredients with ice and
strain into a chilled cocktail, pony or
rocks glass.*

57 T-BIRD

15ml (½ oz) Southern Comfort

15ml (½ oz) Grand Marnier

15ml (½ oz) amaretto

1 splash pineapple juice

ice cubes

*Shake the ingredients with ice and
strain into a chilled cocktail, pony
or rocks glass.*

REVULSION

15ml (½ oz) sambuca

15ml (½ oz) Bailey's Irish Cream

2 drops grenadine

*Layer the liqueurs, in the order given,
in a pony or shot glass. Add the
grenadine by dropping it through a
straw so it flows to the bottom.*

SKIN THE CAT

45ml (1½ oz) Malibu

22ml (¾ oz) 151 rum

1 splash pineapple juice

1 splash cranberry juice

ice cubes

*Shake the Malibu, 151 and pineapple
juice with ice and strain into a
chilled rocks glass. Top up with the
cranberry juice.*

SHOGUN

15ml (½ oz) Midori

37ml (1¼ oz) vodka

Build the ingredients in a pony or shot glass.

SLIPPERY ONE

Equal parts of peppermint schnapps and amaretto

Layer the ingredients, in the order given, in a shot or pony glass.

BANANA SPLIT

Equal parts of crème de banane, crème de almond and Kahlúa

whipped cream

Garnish: maraschino cherry

Layer the ingredients, in the order given, in a pony or shot glass. Top with the whipped cream. Garnish with the cherry.

LIQUID HIGH

Equal parts of Jägermeister, Rumplemintze and Goldschläger

ice cubes

Shake the ingredients with ice and strain into a chilled cocktail, pony or rocks glass.

DEEP THROAT

22ml (¾ oz) vodka

7ml (¼ oz) Tia Maria

whipped cream

Build the ingredients, in the order given, in a pony or shot glass. Top with whipped cream (This drink is taken in one gulp without the use of hands.)

CRANIUM MELTDOWN

7ml (¼ oz) coconut rum

7ml (¼ oz) 151 rum

7ml (¼ oz) Chambord

7ml (¼ oz) pineapple juice

ice cubes

Shake the ingredients with ice and strain into a chilled cocktail, pony or rocks glass.

KEY WASTED

30ml (1oz) Mount Gay

7ml (¼ oz) Cointreau

juice from half a fresh lime

1 dash lime juice

ice cubes

Shake the ingredients with ice and strain into a chilled cocktail, pony or rocks glass.

Jell-o Shots

SWEET TART

| 30ml (1oz) vodka |
| 1 dash Chambord |
| 1 dash lime juice |
| 1 dash pineapple juice |
| ice cubes |

Shake the ingredients with ice and strain into a chilled cocktail, pony or rocks glass.

ROXANNE

| 22ml (¾oz) vodka |
| 22ml (¾oz) peach schnapps |
| 15ml (½oz) amaretto |
| 1 splash cranberry juice |
| 1 splash orange juice |
| ice cubes |

Shake the ingredients with ice and strain into a chilled cocktail, pony or rocks glass.

JELL-O SHOTS

Prepare the Jell-O according to the package with ¾-cup boiling water instead of one. Let cool almost to room temperature. Substitute ¾-cup vodka or other desired spirit for the cold water. Pour into a shot glass and chill.

URINE SAMPLE

| Equal parts of Mount Gay, Malibu, amaretto, orange and pineapple juice |
| ice cubes |

Stir the ingredients with ice and strain into a chilled cocktail, pony or rocks glass.

JACK KNIFE

15ml (½ oz) Jack Daniel's

15ml (½ oz) Bailey's Irish Cream

ice cubes

Shake the ingredients with ice and strain into a shot glass.

ZIPPER

Equal parts of Grand Marnier, tequila and Bailey's Irish Cream

Layer the ingredients, in the order given, in a pony or shot glass.

IRISH FROG

22ml (¾ oz) Midori

22ml (¾ oz) Bailey's Irish Cream (chilled)

Layer the ingredients, in the order given, in a pony or shot glass.

JAGERITA

15ml (½ oz) Jägermeister

15ml (½ oz) Jose Cuervo

15ml (½ oz) Cointreau

1 splash lime juice

ice cubes

Shake the ingredients with ice and strain into a chilled cocktail, pony or rocks glass.

CRYPTO NUGGET

22ml (¾ oz) apple schnapps

15ml (½ oz) vodka

15ml (½ oz) blue curaçao

15ml (½ oz) lime juice

ice cubes

Shake the ingredients with ice and strain into a chilled cocktail, pony or rocks glass.

RUM BALL

30ml (1 oz) Bacardi

22ml (¾ oz) Midori

1 splash orange juice

ice cubes

Shake the ingredients with ice and strain into a chilled cocktail, pony or rocks glass.

PEPPERMINT PATTIE

22ml (¾ oz) peppermint schnapps

15ml (½ oz) Kahlúa

7ml (¼ oz) dark crème de cacao

7ml (¼ oz) vodka

Shake the ingredients with ice and strain into a chilled cocktail, pony or rocks glass.

L'ORANGE ROYALE

Equal parts of orange juice concentrate, Grand Marnier, vodka

1 dash grenadine

Layer the ingredients, in the order given, in a chilled shot or pony glass.

HOLE IN ONE

22ml (¾oz) Midori

7ml (¼oz) apple brandy

1 drop half and half

Layer the ingredients, in the order given, in a pony or shot glass. Using a bar straw, drop the cream into the middle of the shot. Yell 'fore' before shooting it down.

JAMAICAN TENNIS BEADS

15ml (½oz) vodka

15ml (½oz) Malibu

15ml (½oz) crème de banane

15ml (½oz) Chambord

15ml (½oz) pineapple juice

15ml (½oz) half and half

ice cubes

Shake the ingredients with ice and strain into a chilled cocktail, pony or rocks glass. Alternatively, serve on the rocks in a rocks glass.

KAMIKAZE

30ml (1oz) vodka

22ml (¾oz) triple sec

1 dash lime juice

1 dash sour mix

ice cubes

Shake the ingredients with ice and strain into a chilled cocktail, pony or rocks glass.

NEUTRON BOMB

30ml (1oz) beer

10ml (⅓oz) vodka

10ml (⅓oz) rum

10ml (⅓oz) triple sec

10ml (⅓oz) amaretto

10ml (⅓oz) sloe gin

10ml (⅓oz) Galliano

1 dash orange juice

ice cubes

Shake the ingredients with ice and strain into a chilled cocktail glass.

PEACHES AND CREAM

Equal parts of peach schnapps and half and half

1 dash 151 rum

Layer the ingredients, in the order given, in a pony or shot glass.

THE SOMBRERO

Sombrero

60ml (2oz) Kahlúa

60ml (2oz) thick cream

Pour the Kahlúa in a large shot glass. Layer the cream by letting it run down the back of a bar spoon. Serve with a steady hand to avoid disturbing the layers.

KOOL-AID

15ml (½oz) amaretto

15ml (½oz) vodka

15ml (½oz) Midori

1 splash cranberry juice

ice cubes

Shake the ingredients with ice and strain into a chilled cocktail, pony or rocks glass.

FLAMING LAMBORGHINI

30ml (1oz) Kahlúa

30ml (1oz) sambuca

30ml (1oz) blue curaçao and milk (in separate shot glasses)

Combine the Kahlúa and sambuca in a cocktail glass and ignite the mixture. Drink through a straw, and when the drink is almost finished, pour in the blue curaçao and milk, and continue to drink through the straw.

ANGEL'S TIT

Equal parts of dark crème de cacao, maraschino liqueur and thick cream

Garnish: maraschino cherry

Layer the ingredients, in the order given, in a pony glass. Garnish with the cherry.

Angel's Tit

SEAHAWKER

Equal parts of blue curaçao, Midori and vodka

Layer the ingredients, in the order given, in a shot or pony glass.

THREE WISE MEN

Equal parts of Jose Cuervo, Jack Daniel's and Jim Beam

ice cubes

Shake the ingredients with ice and strain into a chilled cocktail, pony or rocks glass.

A-BOMB

Equal parts of Kahlúa, Bailey's Irish Cream, vodka and Tia Maria

ice cubes

Stir the ingredients with ice and strain into a chilled cocktail, pony or rocks glass.

RUSSIAN ROULETTE

2 parts gin

1 part Kahlúa

Float a layer of Kahlúa on top of the gin in a cocktail glass. When the Kahlúa sinks to the bottom, drink up!

SNAKE BITE

30ml (1oz) Seagram's VO

22ml (¾oz) peppermint
schnapps

ice cubes

*Stir the ingredients with ice and
strain into a chilled cocktail, pony
or rocks glass.*

DOUBLE JACK

Equal parts of Jack Daniel's and
Yukon Jack

Build in a pony or shot glass.

SPANISH FLY

Equal parts of amaretto
and tequila

ice cubes

*Shake the ingredients with ice and
strain into a chilled cocktail, pony
or rocks glass.*

ZAMBODIAN SHOOTER

Equal parts of vodka, blackberry
brandy and pineapple juice

ice cubes

*Shake the ingredients with ice and
strain into a chilled cocktail, pony
or rocks glass.*

HOOTER

Equal parts of vodka, amaretto,
grenadine and orange juice

ice cubes

*Shake the ingredients with ice and
strain into a chilled cocktail, pony
or rocks glass.*

WERTHERS

15ml (½oz) vodka

15ml (½oz) butterscotch
schnapps

15ml (½oz) Kahlúa

15ml (½oz) Bailey's Irish Cream

15ml (½oz) white crème
de cacao

1 splash half and half

ice cubes

*Shake the ingredients with ice and
strain into a chilled cocktail, pony
or rocks glass.*

TREE CLIMBER

Equal parts of Southern Comfort,
Kahlúa, amaretto and half
and half

*Shake the ingredients with ice and
strain into a chilled cocktail, pony
or rocks glass.*

DOLLAR BILL

30ml (1oz) rum

30ml (1oz) Midori

1 splash lime juice

ice cubes

Shake the ingredients with ice and strain into a chilled cocktail, pony or rocks glass.

STARBURST

7ml (¼oz) peach schnapps

7ml (¼oz) Chambord

7ml (¼oz) vodka

7ml (¼oz) Midori and Malibu

1 splash sour mix

1 splash cranberry juice

ice cubes

Shake the ingredients with ice and strain into a chilled cocktail, pony or rocks glass.

ABSOLUT QUAALUDE

Equal parts of Absolut vodka, Bailey's Irish Cream and Frangelico

ice cubes

Shake the ingredients with ice and strain into a chilled cocktail, pony or rocks glass.

ALABAMA SLAMMER I (ORIGINAL)

Southern Comfort

1 splash club soda

1 paper napkin

Pour the ingredients into a shot glass or small rocks glass and place the napkin on top. Slam it on the bar, remove the napkin and drink while fizzing.

JEZEBEL

Equal parts of Southern Comfort and Bailey's Irish Cream

Layer the ingredients, in the order given, in a pony or shot glass.

ABC I

Equal parts of amaretto, Bailey's Irish Cream and cognac

Layer the ingredients, in the order given, in a pony or shot glass.

Z-28

Equal parts of white crème de menthe, crème de banane and tequila

Layer the ingredients in, in the order given, in a pony or shot glass.

SKIER ON ACID

Equal parts of Jägermeister
and peach schnapps

1 splash sour mix

1 dash grenadine

ice cubes

*Shake the ingredients with ice and
strain into a chilled cocktail, pony
or rocks glass.*

JELLY DONUT

Equal parts of Chambord and
thick cream

*Layer the ingredients, in the order
given, in a pony or shot glass.*

AVIATION

45ml (1½oz) gin

22ml (¾oz) freshly squeezed
lemon juice

22ml (¾oz) maraschino liqueur

ice cubes

Garnish: twist of lemon and
maraschino cherry (optional)

*Shake the ingredients with ice and
strain into a chilled cocktail, pony
or rocks glass. Garnish with the
twist of lemon and the maraschino
cherry, if preferred.*

ANGEL BLISS

22ml (¾oz) Wild Turkey liqueur

7ml (¼oz) 151 rum

7ml (¼oz) blue curaçao

*Pour the Wild Turkey liqueur into a
pony or shot glass and slowly pour
the rum down the sides of the glass.
Float a layer of curaçao on top.*

B-51

Equal parts of Kahlúa, Bailey's
Irish Cream and 151 rum

*Layer the ingredients, in the order
given, in a shot or pony glass.*

BIT-O-HONEY

Equal parts of apple schnapps
and Frangelico

ice cubes

*Stir the ingredients with ice and
strain into a chilled cocktail, pony
or rocks glass.*

ABC II

Equal parts of amaretto, Bailey's
Irish Cream and Cointreau

*Layer the ingredients, in the order
given, in a pony or shot glass.*

DUCK FART

Equal parts of Kahlúa,
Bailey's Irish Cream and
Crown Royal

*Layer the ingredients, in the order
given, in a shot or pony glass.*

G-BOY

22ml (¾ oz) Bailey's Irish Cream

22ml (¾ oz) Frangelico

22ml (¾ oz) Grand Marnier

ice cubes

*Shake the ingredients with ice and
strain into a chilled cocktail, pony
or rocks glass.*

TRAFFIC LIGHT

Equal parts of grenadine, crème
de banane and green crème
de menthe

*Layer the ingredients, in the order
given, in a pony or large shot glass.*

BUSTED CHERRY

Equal parts of Kahlúa, half and
half and cherry brandy

*Layer the ingredients, in the order
given, in a pony or shot glass.*

FIFTH AVENUE II

Equal parts of dark crème
de cacao, apricot brandy
and half and half

*Layer the ingredients, in the order
given, in a pony or shot glass.*

TRIFECTA

15ml (½ oz) 151 rum

15ml (½ oz) crème de banane

15ml (½ oz) Bailey's Irish Cream

1 dash half and half

ice cubes

*Shake the ingredients with ice and
strain into a chilled cocktail, pony
or rocks glass.*

M AND M

Equal parts of Kahlúa
and amaretto

*Layer the ingredients, in the order
given, in a pony or shot glass.*

WINDSURFER

Equal parts of Kahlúa, triple sec
and Yukon Jack

*Layer the ingredients, in the order
given, in a pony or shot glass.*

BEAM ME UP SCOTTY

Equal parts of Kahlúa, crème de banane and Bailey's Irish Cream

Layer the ingredients, in the order given, in a pony or shot glass.

FREE BASE

Equal parts of Kahlúa and Myers's rum

151 rum

ice cubes

Shake the first five ingredients with ice and strain into a shot or rocks glass. Float a layer of 151 on top. Suck through a straw in one sip.

NUTTY IRISHMAN

Equal parts of Bailey's Irish Cream and Frangelico

ice cubes

Stir the ingredients with ice and strain into a chilled cocktail, pony or rocks glass.

B-57

Equal parts of Kahlúa, triple sec and sambuca

Layer the ingredients, in the order given, in a shot or pony glass.

BUFFALO SWEAT

30ml (1oz) bourbon

1 dash Tabasco sauce

Build the ingredients in a shot glass.

SEX ON THE BEACH

Equal parts of pineapple or cranberry juice, Chambord, peach schnapps and vodka

ice cubes

Build the ingredients in a pony or shot glass, or shake with ice and strain into a chilled cocktail glass.

Sex on the Beach

CHOCOLATE-COVERED CHERRY

Equal parts of grenadine, Kahlúa and Bailey's Irish Cream

Layer the ingredients, in the order given, in a pony or shot glass.

EMBRYO

37ml (1¼oz) peppermint schnapps

1 drop half and half

½ drop grenadine

Pour the schnapps into a pony or shot glass. Run the cream and grenadine down a straw into the middle of the shot.

WHITE SPIDER

Equal parts of white crème de menthe and white crème de cacao

Layer the ingredients, in the order given, in a pony or shot glass.

CUCARACHA

15ml (½oz) Kahlúa

30ml (1oz) tequila

Build, in the order given, in a rocks glass. Ignite and drink with a straw.

DR PEPPER

30ml (1oz) amaretto

151 rum

1 glass beer

Pour amaretto into a shot glass and top with rum. Drop the mixture into the beer. Note: Set the shot alight before dropping it into the beer for a Flaming Dr Pepper.

NEUTRON

60ml (2oz) vodka

15ml (½oz) Midori

1 dash blue curaçao

1 dash lemon-lime soda

ice cubes

Shake the ingredients with ice and strain into a chilled cocktail, pony or rocks glass.

LIQUID VALIUM

Equal parts of Jim Beam and peach schnapps

1 splash cranberry juice

1 splash orange juice

ice cubes

Shake the ingredients with ice and strain into a chilled cocktail, pony or rocks glass.

BABY, BABY, BABY

30ml (1oz) Stolichnaya
Razberi vodka

22ml (¾oz) Grand Marnier

15ml (½oz) Bailey's Irish Cream

ice cubes

Stir the ingredients with ice and strain into a chilled cocktail, pony or rocks glass.

SURFER ON ACID

37ml (1¼oz) Malibu

37ml (1¼oz) Jägermeister

1 splash pineapple juice

ice cubes

Shake the ingredients with ice and strain into a chilled cocktail, pony or rocks glass.

TEST TUBE II

30ml (1oz) Wild Turkey liqueur

15ml (½oz) peppermint schnapps

1 drop Bailey's Irish Cream

Layer the liqueur and schnapps in a large shot glass. Drop the Bailey's into the shot using a hollow swizzle stick.

RUSSIAN QUAALUDE

Equal parts of Bailey's Irish Cream, Frangelico and vodka

ice cubes

Shake the ingredients with ice. Strain into a chilled cocktail or rocks glass.

IRISH QUAALUDE

Equal parts of vodka, Bailey's Irish Cream, Frangelico and white crème de cacao

ice cubes

Shake the ingredients with ice and strain into a chilled cocktail, pony or rocks glass.

BLACK SAND

15ml (½oz) Kahlúa

15ml (½oz) black sambuca

15ml (½oz) amaretto

Layer the ingredients, in the order given, in a pony or shot glass.

EARTHQUAKE

Equal parts of amaretto, sambuca and Southern Comfort

Layer the ingredients, in the order given, in a pony or shot glass.

NUTCRACKER

2 parts Frangelico

1 part amaretto or vodka

half and half

Pour the Frangelico into a shot glass and float a layer of amaretto on top. Finish with a layer of half and half.

TROPICAL LIFESAVER

30ml (1oz) Absolut Citron

15ml (½oz) Midori

15ml (½oz) Malibu

1 splash sour mix

1 splash pineapple juice

ice cubes

Shake the ingredients with ice and strain into a chilled cocktail, pony or rocks glass.

BLOODY BOOGER

30ml (1oz) Midori (chilled)

1 dash Chambord

Bailey's Irish Cream

Pour the Midori into a chilled cocktail glass. Gently drop the Chambord into the Midori and let it sink to the bottom. Float a layer of Bailey's on top.

Nutcracker

BUSHWHACKER

7ml (¼oz) white crème de cacao

7ml (¼oz) cream of coconut

7ml (¼oz) Kahlúa

7ml (¼oz) 151 rum

7ml (¼oz) half and half

ice cubes

Shake the ingredients with ice and strain into a chilled cocktail, pony or rocks glass.

GRAPE CRUSH

Equal parts of vodka
and Chambord

1 splash sour mix

1 dash lemon-lime soda

*Shake the ingredients and strain into
a chilled cocktail, pony or rocks
glass. Top up with the soda.*

KEY LIME PIE

45ml (1½oz) Licor 43

1 splash lime juice

1 splash half and half

*Shake the ingredients with ice and
strain into a chilled cocktail, pony
or rocks glass.*

CANADIAN MOOSE

Equal parts of Kahlúa,
Bailey's Irish Cream
and Crown Royal

*Layer the ingredients, in the order
given, in a pony or shot glass.*

NINJA

Equal parts of dark crème de
cacao, Frangelico and Midori

*Layer the ingredients, in the order
given, in a pony or shot glass.*

BUTTERY NIPPLE

Equal parts of butterscotch
schnapps and Bailey's
Irish Cream

*Layer the ingredients, in the order
given, in a large cordial or shot glass.*

NUCLEAR ACCELERATOR

Equal parts of peppermint
schnapps, Grand Marnier
and vodka

*Layer the ingredients, in the order
given, in a pony or shot glass.*

CEMENT MIXER

Bailey's Irish Cream and
lime juice

*Serve each ingredient separately,
in shot glasses – first the Bailey's
then the lime juice. Swirl both in
the mouth before swallowing.*

ADAM BOMB

Equal parts of apple schnapps
and Goldschläger

ice cubes

*Shake the ingredients with ice and
strain into a chilled cocktail, pony
or rocks glass.*

RED SNAPPER

Equal parts of Crown Royal,
peach schnapps and
cranberry juice

ice cubes

*Shake the ingredients with ice and
strain into a chilled cocktail, pony
or rocks glass.*

PURPLE HAZE

Equal parts of vodka
and Chambord

1 dash sour mix

1 dash cranberry juice

ice cubes

*Shake the ingredients with ice and
strain into a chilled cocktail, pony
or rocks glass.*

CARIBBEAN BERRY

15ml (½oz) Myers's rum

7ml (¼oz) coconut rum

7ml (¼oz) Midori

7ml (¼oz) peach schnapps

7ml (¼oz) cranberry juice

ice cubes

*Shake the ingredients with ice and
strain into a chilled cocktail, pony
or rocks glass.*

WHIPSTER

Equal parts of dark crème de
cacao, apricot brandy and
triple sec

*Layer the ingredients, in the order
given, in a pony or shot glass.*

VAMPIRE

37ml (1¼oz) vodka

22ml (¾oz) Chambord

1 splash cranberry juice

ice cubes

*Shake the ingredients with ice and
strain into a chilled cocktail, pony
or rocks glass.*

BLACK FOREST CAKE

Equal parts of cherry brandy,
Kahlúa and Bailey's Irish Cream

ice cubes

*Shake the brandy and Kahlúa
with ice and strain into a pony
or shot glass. Float a layer of
Bailey's on top.*

DAGGER

Equal parts of tequila, dark crème de cacao and peppermint schnapps

Layer the ingredients, in the order given, in a pony or shot glass.

FREDDY KRUGER

Equal parts of sambuca, Jägermeister and vodka

Layer the ingredients, in the order given, in a shot or pony glass.

HARBOUR LIGHTS

Equal parts of Kahlúa, tequila and 151 rum

Layer the ingredients, in the order given, in a pony or shot glass.

ITALIAN PECKER

15ml (½ oz) Mozart

7ml (¼oz) Myers's rum cream

7ml (¼ oz) Galliano

7ml (¼ oz) Tuaca

ice cubes

Shake the ingredients with ice and strain into a chilled cocktail, pony or rocks glass.

B-52

Equal parts of Kahlúa, Bailey's Irish Cream and Grand Marnier

Pour the Kahlúa into a pony glass and gently float the Bailey's on top. Finish with a layer of Grand Marnier.

B52

BJ

GREEK REVOLUTION

Equal parts of grenadine, ouzo and Galliano

Layer the ingredients, in the order given, in a pony or shot glass.

HARD ONE

22ml (¾ oz) vodka

15ml (½ oz) Frangelico

1 splash club soda

Shake the ingredients and pour into a chilled cocktail, pony or rocks glass.

AFTER EIGHT

Equal parts of Kahlúa, white crème de menthe and Bailey's Irish Cream

Layer the ingredients, in the order given, in a pony or shot glass.

BJ

Equal parts of Kahlúa and Bailey's Irish Cream

whipped cream (optional)

Pour the Kahlúa in a pony or shot glass. Float a layer of Bailey's on top. Finish with the whipped cream, if desired. This drink is taken in one gulp without using your hands.

CARROT CAKE

Equal parts of Goldschläger, butterscotch schnapps and Bailey's Irish Cream

ice cubes

Shake the ingredients with ice and strain into a chilled cocktail, pony or rocks glass.

GEORGIA PEACH

Equal parts of peach schnapps
and Southern Comfort

ice cubes

*Shake the ingredients with ice and
strain into a chilled cocktail, pony
or rocks glass.*

FIVE-DOLLAR MARGARET

22ml (¾ oz) Chambord

22ml (¾ oz) Kahlúa

22ml (¾ oz) amaretto

22ml (¾ oz) half and half

ice cubes

*Shake the ingredients with ice and
strain into a chilled cocktail, pony
or rocks glass.*

BLACK ORCHID

30ml (1oz) Bacardi black

30ml (1oz) Chambord

15ml (½ oz) grenadine

15ml (½ oz) cranberry juice

1 splash lemon-lime soda

ice cubes

*Shake all the ingredients, except the
soda, with ice. Strain into a chilled
rocks glass. Top up with soda.*

PEACE IN IRELAND

Equal parts of Irish Mist and
Bailey's Irish Cream

ice cubes

*Shake the ingredients with ice and
strain into a chilled cocktail, pony
or rocks glass.*

HAWAIIAN

Equal parts of vodka, amaretto
and cranberry juice

ice cubes

*Shake the ingredients with ice and
strain into a chilled cocktail, pony
or rocks glass.*

JOLLY GREEN GIANT

Equal parts of rum, gin, tequila,
blue curaçao and Galliano

ice cubes

*Stir ingredients with ice. Strain into a
chilled cocktail, pony or rocks glass.*

AFTER-FIVE SHOOTER

Equal parts of Kahlúa,
Bailey's Irish Cream and
peppermint schnapps

*Layer the ingredients, in the order
given, in a pony or shot glass.*

TIGHT SNATCH

15ml (½ oz) Malibu

15ml (½ oz) Bacardi

15ml (½ oz) peach schnapps

1 splash pineapple juice

1 splash cranberry juice

ice cubes

Shake the ingredients with ice and strain into a chilled cocktail, pony or rocks glass.

DELLEN DELIGHT

Equal parts of Jägermeister, pineapple juice and Myers's rum

ice cubes

Shake the ingredients with ice and strain into a chilled cocktail, pony or rocks glass.

ESKIMO KISS

Equal parts of amaretto, cherry brandy and Swiss Chocolate Almond

whipped cream

Layer the ingredients, in the order given, in a pony or shot glass. Top with the whipped cream.

FIFTH AVENUE I

Equal parts of Bailey's Irish Cream, Kahlúa and peppermint schnapps

Layer the ingredients, in the order given, in a pony or shot glass.

BLUE POPPER

30ml (1oz) tequila

7ml (¼ oz) blue curaçao

Layer the ingredients in a pony glass.

GREEN SNEAKER

60ml (2oz) vodka

15ml (½ oz) Midori

15ml (½ oz) triple sec

1 splash orange juice

Stir the ingredients with ice and strain into a chilled cocktail, pony or rocks glass.

ABSOLUT NUT

30ml (1oz) Absolut vodka

30ml (1oz) Frangelico

ice cubes

Shake the ingredients with ice and strain into a chilled cocktail, pony or rocks glass. Alternatively, serve on the rocks.

VO BREEZE

Equal parts of grenadine, peppermint schnapps and Seagram's VO

Layer the ingredients, in the order given, in a pony or shot glass.

B-53

Equal parts of Kahlúa, Bailey's Irish Cream, Grand Marnier and vodka

Layer the ingredients, in the order given, in a shot or pony glass.

LIFESAVER (MIXED FRUIT)

45ml (1½oz) crème de banane

15ml (½oz) blackberry brandy

ice cubes

Shake the ingredients with ice and strain into a chilled cocktail, pony or rocks glass.

BANANA BOAT

Equal parts of Tia Maria, Kahlúa, peppermint schnapps and Myers's rum cream

Layer the ingredients, in the order given, in a pony or shot glass.

PURPLE RAIN

45ml (1½oz) vodka

1 splash blue curaçao

1 splash cranberry juice

ice cubes

Stir the ingredients with ice and strain into a chilled cocktail, pony or rocks glass.

THE BRAIN

22ml (¾oz) strawberry schnapps

1 dash grenadine

Bailey's Irish Cream (chilled)

ice cubes

Stir the strawberry schnapps with ice and strain into a large shot glass. Add the dash of grenadine and gently float a layer of Bailey's on top.

HONEY DEW

Equal parts of Barenjäger and Midori

1 splash pineapple juice

ice cubes

Shake the ingredients with ice and strain into a chilled cocktail, pony or rocks glass.

CHOCOLATE CHIP

Equal parts of Swiss Chocolate
Almond, dark crème de cacao
and Bailey's Irish Cream

*Layer the ingredients, in the order
given, in a pony or shot glass.*

JELLY BEAN

Equal parts of blackberry
brandy and anisette

*Layer the ingredients, in the order
given, in a pony or shot glass.
Alternatively, build and serve on
the rocks.*

NIGHTMARE

Equal parts of Jägermeister, 151
rum and Goldschläger

ice cubes

*Shake the ingredients with ice and
strain into a chilled cocktail, pony
or rocks glass.*

FIREBALL

22ml (¾oz) cinnamon
schnapps

7ml (¼oz) cherry brandy

*Layer the ingredients, in the order
given, in a pony or shot glass.*

CHOCOLATE BANANA

Equal parts of dark crème de
cacao and crème de banane

ice cubes

*Shake the ingredients with ice and
strain into a chilled cocktail, pony
or rocks glass.*

GERMAN CHOCOLATE
CAKE

15ml (½oz) Jägermeister

15ml (½oz) chocolate liqueur

7ml (¼oz) coconut rum

7ml (¼oz) butterscotch
schnapps

ice cubes

*Shake the ingredients with ice and
strain into a pony or shot glass.*

NEW YORK NUTTY

1 dash vodka

1 dash amaretto

1 dash Frangelico

1 dash Tia Maria

1 splash half and half

ice cubes

*Shake the ingredients with ice and
strain into a chilled cocktail, pony
or rocks glass.*

MELON BALL SHOOTER

Equal parts of vodka, Midori and pineapple or orange juice

Pour the vodka into a shot glass and add a layer of Midori. Top with a layer of fresh pineapple or orange juice.

LIQUID PLEASURE

Equal parts of Jägermeister, Rumplemintze and sambuca

ice cubes

Shake the ingredients with ice and strain into a chilled cocktail, pony or rocks glass.

Melon Ball Shooter

WENCH

Equal parts of amaretto and Captain Morgan

ice cubes

Shake the ingredients with ice and strain into a chilled cocktail, pony or rocks glass.

MAD COW

Equal parts of Kahlúa, half and half, and 151 rum

Shake the ingredients with ice and strain into a chilled cocktail, pony or rocks glass.

F-52

Equal parts of Kahlúa, Bailey's Irish Cream and Frangelico

Layer the ingredients, in the order given, in a pony or shot glass.

ALABAMA SLAMMER II

15ml (½ oz) Southern Comfort

15ml (½ oz) amaretto

15ml (½ oz) sloe gin

1 splash orange or lemon juice

ice cubes

Shake the ingredients with ice and strain into a chilled cocktail, pony or rocks glass.

NEW YORK SLAMMER

15ml (½ oz) Southern Comfort

15ml (½ oz) amaretto

15ml (½ oz) triple sec

15ml (½ oz) sloe gin

15ml (½ oz) orange juice

ice cubes

Shake the ingredients with ice and strain into a chilled cocktail, pony or rocks glass.

AMBUSH

30ml (1 oz) Bushmills

30ml (1 oz) amaretto

ice cubes

Shake the ingredients with ice and strain into a chilled cocktail, pony or rocks glass.

Angel's Kiss

ANGEL'S KISS

7ml (¼ oz) sloe gin

7ml (¼ oz) brandy

7ml (¼ oz) white crème de cacao

7ml (¼ oz) half and half

Pour the crème de cacao in a shot glass, float a layer of sloe gin and then the brandy on top. Finish with a layer of cream.

JAMAICAN DUST

Equal parts of 151 rum, Tia
Maria and pineapple juice

ice cubes

*Shake the ingredients with ice and
strain into a chilled cocktail, pony
or rocks glass.*

TOOTSIE ROLL SHOOTER

Equal parts of Mozart or chocolate liqueur, dark crème de
cacao and half and half

*Layer the ingredients, in the order
given, in a pony or shot glass.*

WARM BLONDE

Equal parts of Southern Comfort
and amaretto

*Layer the ingredients, in the order
given, in a pony or shot glass.*

RED-HEADED HOTTIE I

Equal parts of Chambord, Crown
Royal and Southern Comfort

ice cubes

*Shake the ingredients with ice and
strain into a chilled cocktail, pony
or rocks glass.*

IRISH HEADLOCK

Equal parts of brandy, amaretto,
Bailey's Irish Cream and
Irish whiskey

*Layer the ingredients, in the order
given, in a pony or shot glass.*

ANDES CANDIES

Equal parts of dark crème
de cacao and green crème
de menthe

*Layer the ingredients, in the order
given, in a pony or shot glass.*

WATERMELON

Equal parts of vodka, Midori
and cranberry juice

ice cubes

*Shake the ingredients with ice and
strain into a chilled cocktail, pony
or rocks glass.*

CINNAMON TOAST

Equal parts of Bailey's Irish
Cream and Goldschläger

ice cubes

*Shake the ingredients with ice and
strain into a chilled cocktail, pony
or rocks glass.*

KRYPTONITE

15ml (½ oz) vodka	
15ml (½ oz) Malibu	
15ml (½ oz) peach schnapps	
15ml (½ oz) blue curaçao	
15ml (½ oz) Midori	
1 splash pineapple juice	
1 dash grenadine	
ice cubes	

Shake the ingredients with ice and strain into a chilled cocktail, pony or rocks glass.

VOODOO SHOOTER

Equal parts of Tia Maria, Myers's rum cream and 151 rum

Layer the ingredients, in the order given, in a shot or pony glass.

POUSSE CAFÉ

1 part red grenadine
1 part Cointreau
1 part green crème de menthe
1 part Galliano
1 part dark brandy

Pour the grenadine in a shot glass. Float a layer of Cointreau, crème de menthe and Galliano on top. Finish with a layer of brandy.

COUGH DROP

Equal parts of blackberry brandy and peppermint schnapps

Build the ingredients in a shot or pony glass.

BIKINI LINE

Equal parts of Chambord, Tia Maria and vodka

Layer the ingredients, in the order given, in a pony or shot glass.

Pousse Café

PANTHER

Equal parts of peach brandy and white crème de menthe

ice cubes

Stir the ingredients with ice and strain into a chilled cocktail, pony or rocks glass.

TIDY BOWL

45ml (1½oz) vodka

1 dash blue curaçao

raisins

ice cubes

Shake the vodka and blue curaçao with ice. Strain the mixture into a small round glass. Drop a couple of raisins in the bottom.

BEAUTIFUL

Equal parts of Grand Marnier and Courvoisier

Layer the ingredients, in the order given, in a pony or shot glass.

EASTER EGG SHOOTER

Equal parts of Chambord, Tia Maria and half and half

Layer the ingredients, in the order given, in a pony or shot glass.

BOTTOM BOUNCER

Equal parts of Bailey's Irish Cream and butterscotch schnapps

ice cubes

Pour the ingredients over ice in a rocks glass, or swirl over ice and strain into a chilled cocktail, pony or rocks glass.

JEKYLL AND HYDE

15ml (½oz) Jägermeister

15ml (½oz) peppermint schnapps

ice cubes

Shake the ingredients with ice and strain into a shot glass. Alternatively, serve on the rocks.

JOLLY RANCHER

22ml (¾oz) vodka

7ml (¼oz) Midori

7ml (¼oz) peach schnapps

1 splash cranberry juice

ice cubes

Shake the ingredients with ice and strain into a chilled cocktail, pony or rocks glass.

PAINLESS

22ml (¾ oz) Bailey's Irish Cream

22ml (¾ oz) Crown Royal

22ml (¾ oz) amaretto

ice cubes

Shake the ingredients with ice and serve in a rocks glass.

RASPBERRY BERET

Equal parts of vodka, Chambord and half and half

1 splash club soda

ice cubes

Shake the ingredients with ice and strain into a chilled cocktail, pony or rocks glass.

GOOD AND PLENTY

Equal parts of Kahlúa and ouzo

Layer the ingredients, in the order given, in a pony or shot glass.

AUNT JEMIMA

Equal parts of white crème de cacao, brandy and Benedictine

Layer the ingredients, in the order given, in a pony or shot glass.

PEACH SLINGSHOT

Equal parts of peach schnapps, gin and sour mix

1 dash grenadine

ice cubes

Shake the ingredients with ice and strain into a chilled cocktail, pony or rocks glass.

DC-9

Equal parts of Kahlúa, sambuca and Myers's rum cream

Layer the ingredients, in the order given, in a pony or shot glass.

CHOCOLATE MONK

Equal parts of Kahlúa, Frangelico and Bailey's Irish Cream

Layer the ingredients, in the order given, in a pony or shot glass.

PUPPY'S NOSE

Equal parts of peppermint schnapps, Tia Maria and Bailey's Irish Cream

Build the schnapps and Tia Maria in a pony or shot glass. Float a layer of Bailey's on top.

KING ALPHONSE

30ml (1oz) dark crème
de cacao

whipped cream

Garnish: maraschino cherry

*Layer the cream on top of the crème
de cacao in a pony glass. Spear a
cocktail pick through a cherry and
place it on top of the glass.*

AMERICAN FLAG

Equal parts of grenadine, blue
curaçao and half and half

*Layer the ingredients, in the order
given, in a pony or shot glass.*

PINEAPPLE BOMB

30ml (1oz) Southern Comfort

15ml (½oz) amaretto

1 splash pineapple juice

ice cubes

*Shake the ingredients with ice and
strain into a chilled cocktail, pony or
rocks glass.*

BOB MARLEY

Equal parts of red grenadine,
Advokaat egg cream and green
crème de menthe

*Layer the ingredients, in the order
given, in a shot glass.*

CHAMBORD KAMIKAZE

37ml (1¼oz) vodka

1 splash Chambord

1 splash sour mix

1 splash simple syrup

ice cubes

*Shake the ingredients with ice and
strain into a chilled cocktail, pony
or rocks glass.*

Bob Marley

TIDAL WAVE

Equal parts of 151 rum,
Captain Morgan and vodka

1 splash sour mix

1 splash cranberry juice

ice cubes

Shake the ingredients with ice and strain into a chilled cocktail, pony or rocks glass.

BERTIE BICHBERG

Equal parts of crème de banane, Bailey's Irish Cream and vodka

Garnish: maraschino cherry

Pour the ingredients into a pony or shot glass. Drop the cherry into the glass, pull it out, shoot down the drink, then eat the cherry.

SILENT MONK

30ml (1oz) Benedictine

15ml (½oz) triple sec

1 splash half and half

ice cubes

Shake the ingredients with ice and strain into a chilled cocktail, pony or rocks glass.

LIQUORICE STICK

30ml (1oz) vodka

15ml (½oz) anisette

15ml (½oz) triple sec

ice cubes

Shake the ingredients with ice and strain into a chilled cocktail, pony or rocks glass.

OATMEAL COOKIE

22ml (¾oz) butterscotch schnapps

22ml (¾oz) Bailey's Irish Cream

1 dash Jägermeister

1 dash cinnamon schnapps

Garnish: raisins

Shake the ingredients with ice and strain into a chilled cocktail, pony or rocks glass. Alternatively, serve on the rocks. Garnish with skewered raisins.

DEPTH CHARGE

spearmint or peppermint schnapps

½ glass draught beer

Drop a shot of schnapps into the beer and drink up.

TOXIC WASTE

15ml (½oz) Southern Comfort

15ml (½oz) Midori

15ml (½oz) Stolichnaya Razberi

1 splash cranberry juice

1 dash sour mix

ice cubes

Shake the ingredients with ice and strain into a chilled cocktail, pony or rocks glass.

SCREAMING EAGLE

Equal parts of Jägermeister and Rumplemintze or Goldschläger

ice cubes

Shake the ingredients with ice and strain into a chilled cocktail, pony or rocks glass.

JÄGER BOMB

37ml (1¼oz) Jägermeister

½ can Red Bull

Drop the Jägermeister into a chilled glass of Red Bull. Alternatively, substitute Black Haus liqueur for another variation called a Black Bull.)

HEAD ROOM

7ml (¼oz) crème de banane

7ml (¼oz) Midori

15ml (½oz) Bailey's Irish Cream

Layer the ingredients, in the order given, in a pony or shot glass.

ADDICTIVE

Equal parts of blackberry brandy and vodka

1 splash grapefruit juice

ice cubes

Shake the ingredients with ice and strain into a chilled cocktail, pony or rocks glass.

FACE DOWN

Equal parts of amaretto, triple sec, blackberry brandy and lime juice

Layer the ingredients, in the order given, in a pony or large shot glass.

RAINBOW

Equal parts of crème de noyaux, crème de banane, blue curaçao, Midori and half and half

Layer the ingredients, in the order given, in a pony or shot glass.

MUDSLIDE

Equal parts of Kahlúa, Bailey's
Irish Cream and vodka

*Layer the ingredients, in the order
given, in a pony or shot glass.*

SOUTHERN BEACH

30ml (1oz) Southern Comfort
15ml (½oz) peach schnapps
7ml (¼oz) crème de noyaux
1 splash orange juice
1 dash pineapple
1 dash cranberry juice
ice cubes

*Shake the ingredients with ice and
strain into a chilled cocktail, pony
or rocks glass.*

OLD LAY

37ml (1¼oz) Jose Cuervo
22ml (¾oz) triple sec
1 splash lime juice
1 splash grenadine
ice cubes

*Shake the ingredients with ice and
strain into a chilled cocktail, pony
or rocks glass. Top with a dash
of grenadine.*

Mudslide

MILES OF SMILES

15ml (½oz) Canadian Club
15ml (½oz) peppermint schnapps
15ml (½oz) amaretto
ice cubes

*Stir the ingredients with ice and
strain into a chilled cocktail, pony
or rocks glass.*

NUTTY JAMAICAN

30ml (1oz) Myers's rum cream

15ml (½ oz) Frangelico

ice cubes

Stir the ingredients with ice and strain into a chilled cocktail, pony or rocks glass.

KITCHEN SINK

22ml (¾ oz) amaretto

22ml (¾ oz) orange curaçao

1 dash orange juice

1 dash pineapple juice

1 dash sour mix

ice cubes

Shake the ingredients with ice and strain into a chilled cocktail, pony or rocks glass.

TIE ME TO THE BEDPOST

15ml (½ oz) Midori

15ml (½ oz) Absolut Citron

15ml (½ oz) Malibu

1 splash sour mix

Shake the ingredients with ice and strain into a chilled cocktail, pony or rocks glass.

SPACE PUSSY

Equal parts of Malibu and raspberry vodka

1 splash sour mix

1 splash lemon-lime soda

15ml (½ oz) Chambord or blue curaçao

ice cubes

Shake the Malibu, vodka, sour mix and soda with ice and strain into a chilled cocktail, pony or rocks glass. Sink the Chambord or blue curaçao to the bottom of the glass.

207

CHAMBORD ADRENALIN

Equal parts of Chambord and Absolut vodka

ice cubes

Shake the ingredients with ice and strain into a chilled cocktail, pony or rocks glass.

T.K.O.

Equal parts of tequila, Kahlúa and ouzo

ice cubes

Shake the ingredients with ice and strain into a chilled cocktail, pony or rocks glass.

RASPBERRY KISS

Equal parts of Chambord,
Kahlúa and half and half

ice cubes

*Shake the ingredients with ice and
strain into a chilled cocktail, pony
or rocks glass.*

DC-3

Equal parts of dark crème de
cacao, sambuca and Bailey's
Irish Cream

*Layer the ingredients, in the order
given, in a pony or shot glass.*

ROCK LOBSTER

Equal parts of Chambord, Crown
Royal and cranberry juice

ice cubes

*Shake the ingredients with ice and
strain into a chilled cocktail, pony
or rocks glass.*

E.T.

Equal parts of Midori, Bailey's
Irish Cream and vodka

*Layer the ingredients, in the order
given, in a pony or shot glass.*

ORANGE CRUSH

Equal parts of vodka, triple sec
and orange juice

ice cubes

*Shake the ingredients with ice and
strain into a chilled cocktail, pony
or rocks glass.*

DANGEROUS LIAISONS

Equal parts of Tia Maria
and Cointreau

1 splash sour mix

ice cubes

*Shake the ingredients with ice and
strain into a chilled cocktail, pony
or rocks glass.*

MEMPHIS BELLE

Equal parts of Southern Comfort
and Bailey's Irish Cream

*Shake the ingredients with ice and
strain into a chilled cocktail, pony
or rocks glass.*

ROCKET FUEL

Equal parts of Rumplemintze
and 151 rum

*Layer the ingredients, in the order
given, in a shot or pony glass.*

STAR WARS

Equal parts of amaretto,
Southern Comfort, triple
sec and grenadine

ice cubes

*Shake the ingredients with ice and
strain into a chilled cocktail, pony
or rocks glass.*

NYMPHOMANIAC

30ml (1oz) Captain Morgan

7ml (¼oz) peach schnapps

7ml (¼oz) Malibu

ice cubes

*Shake the ingredients with ice and
strain into a chilled cocktail, pony
or rocks glass.*

MONKEY GLAND

45ml (1½oz) gin

1 splash orange juice

1 dash Benedictine

1 dash grenadine

ice cubes

*Shake the ingredients with ice and
strain into a chilled cocktail, pony
or rocks glass.*

Jellyfish

JELLYFISH

Equal parts of dark crème de
cacao, amaretto and Bailey's
Irish Cream

1 drop grenadine

*Pour the crème de cacao into a shot
glass. Carefully add a layer of
amaretto and then the Bailey's. Using
a hollow stir stick, drop a little grenadine on the top layer.*

SWEET PEACH

30ml (1oz) amaretto

22ml (¾oz) peach schnapps

15ml (½oz) orange juice

ice cubes

Shake the ingredients with ice and strain into a chilled cocktail, pony or rocks glass.

Slippery Nipple

SLIPPERY NIPPLE

Equal parts of black sambuca and Bailey's Irish Cream

Layer the ingredients, in the order given, in a shot glass.

LOBOTOMY

Equal parts of amaretto, Chambord, pineapple juice and champagne

ice cubes

Shake the ingredients with ice and strain into a chilled cocktail, pony or rocks glass.

MEXICAN BERRY

22ml (¾oz) Chambord

7ml (¼oz) Jose Cuervo gold

ice cubes

Shake the ingredients with ice and strain into a sugar-frosted pony glass.

EIGHT SECONDS

Equal parts of Jägermeister, Goldschläger, Hot Damn and Rumplemintze

Shake the ingredients with ice and strain into a chilled cocktail, pony or rocks glass.

T-SHOT

Equal parts of white crème de cacao, Tia Maria, Bailey's Irish Cream and half and half

Layer the ingredients, in the order given, in a pony or shot glass.

PANCHO VILLA

Equal parts of crème de noyaux, green Chartreuse, Jose Cuervo and 151 rum

Layer the ingredients, in the order given, in a pony or shot glass.

JACK AND JILL

Equal parts of Jack Daniel's and rootbeer schnapps

ice cubes

Stir the ingredients with ice and strain into a chilled cocktail, pony or rocks glass.

GREEN GENIE

Equal parts of green Chartreuse and tequila

ice cubes

Stir the ingredients over ice and strain into a chilled cocktail, pony or rocks glass.

TEXAS SWEAT

Equal parts of grenadine, green crème de menthe, Jose Cuervo and Bacardi rum

Layer the ingredients, in the order given, in a pony or shot glass.

LETHAL INJECTION

Equal parts of Malibu, Captain Morgan, Bacardi black and crème de noyaux

1 splash orange juice

1 splash pineapple juice

ice cubes

Shake the ingredients with ice and strain into a chilled cocktail, pony or rocks glass.

RASPBERRY GRENADE

Equal parts of Chambord peach schnapps, vodka and lime juice

Shake the ingredients with ice and strain into a chilled cocktail, pony or rocks glass.

LOUISIANA BAYOU

Equal parts of Kahlúa, Midori and Bailey's Irish Cream

Layer the ingredients, in the order given, in a pony or shot glass.

QUAALUDE

Equal parts of Bailey's Irish Cream, Grand Marnier and vodka

ice cubes

Stir the ingredients with ice and strain into a chilled cocktail, pony or rocks glass.

MEXICAN FLAG

Equal parts of grenadine, green crème de menthe and Bailey's Irish Cream

Layer the ingredients, in the order given, in a pony or shot glass.

PEANUT BUTTER AND JELLY

Equal parts of Frangelico, Chambord and half and half

ice cubes

Shake the ingredients with ice and strain into a chilled cocktail, pony or rocks glass.

PURPLE NURPLE

15ml (½ oz) tequila

7ml (¼ oz) blue curaçao

7ml (¼ oz) sloe gin

ice cubes

Stir the ingredients with ice and strain into a chilled cocktail, pony or rocks glass.

RED-HEADED HOTTIE II

Equal parts of Jägermeister, peach schnapps and cranberry juice

ice cubes

Shake the ingredients with ice and strain into a chilled cocktail, pony or rocks glass.

ROYAL FLUSH

30ml (1oz) Crown Royal

22ml (¾ oz) peach schnapps

15 ml (½ oz) Chambord

1 splash cranberry juice

Shake the ingredients with ice and strain into a chilled cocktail, pony or rocks glass.

MANGLED FROG

22ml (¾oz) Midori

15ml (½oz) Bailey's
Irish Cream

1 dash grenadine

Float the Bailey's on top of the Midori in a pony or shot glass. Drop the grenadine down the middle of the shot using a straw.

Mangled Frog

SWEDISH FISH

Equal parts of Black
Haus liqueur and sour mix

1 splash cranberry juice

ice cubes

Shake ingredients with ice. Strain into a chilled cocktail, pony or rocks glass.

SOUTHERN SUICIDE

22ml (¾oz) Jack Daniel's

22ml (¾oz) Southern Comfort

15ml (½oz) orange juice

7ml (¼oz) grenadine

7ml (¼oz) lemon-lime soda

ice cubes

Shake the ingredients with ice and strain into a chilled cocktail, pony or rocks glass.

CARAMEL APPLE

Equal parts of butterscotch
schnapps and Apple Puckers

ice cubes

Shake with ice and strain into a chilled cocktail, pony or rocks glass.

MAT COCKTAIL

The spillage mat at the end of the night

Line up the shot glasses and pour!
(Also known as a LA Freeway)

HOLIDAYS AND OCCASIONS

The holidays are a time for celebration and sharing good times with family and friends. Traditions exist among different cultures, which were passed through generations. Many have changed from the original intentions into customs sometimes far removed from their initial purpose. Yet, getting together and commemorating a special occasion is still a good time to drink and toast in remembrances of holidays past, and making new memories to reflect upon for years to come.

New Year

'May friendship, like wine, improve as time advances, and may we always have old wine, old friends, and young cares.'

CHAMPAGNE COCKTAIL

1 dash bitters

1 dash simple syrup

champagne (chilled) to fill

Garnish: twist of lemon

Pour the dashes of bitters and simple syrup into a champagne glass. Fill with champagne and garnish with the twist of lemon.

Chinese New Year

'An inch of time is an inch of gold, but you can't buy that inch of time with an inch of gold.'

SCORPION BOWL

180ml (6oz) Puerto Rican rum

180ml (6oz) orange juice

120ml (4oz) lemon juice

45ml (1½oz) orgeat syrup

30ml (1oz) brandy

2 cups crushed ice

ice cubes

Garnish: gardenia

Blend the ingredients with the crushed ice and pour the mixture into a bowl. Add ice cubes to fill the bowl and garnish with a gardenia. Makes 2–4 servings.

Birthday

'Another candle on your cake? Well, that's no cause to pout. Be glad that you have strength enough, to blow the damned things out.'

SKIP AND GO NAKED

30ml (1oz) gin

1 dash grenadine

1 splash sour mix

1 splash draft beer

ice cubes

Shake the ingredients with ice. Strain into a chilled cocktail or rocks glass.

St. Patrick's Day

'May you have warm words on a cold evening, a full moon on a dark night, and the road downhill all the way to your door.'

Blarney Stone Cocktail

BLARNEY STONE SOUR

45ml (1½oz) Irish whiskey
1 splash orange juice
1 splash sour mix
ice cubes
Garnish: orange wheel and maraschino cherry

Shake the ingredients with ice and strain into a chilled flute. Garnish with a flag.

EVERYBODY'S IRISH COCKTAIL

60ml (2oz) Irish whiskey
1 tsp green Chartreuse
1 tsp green crème de menthe
ice cubes
Garnish: olive

Stir the ingredients with ice and strain into a chilled cocktail glass. Garnish with the olive.

BLARNEY STONE COCKTAIL

60ml (2oz) Irish whiskey
½ tsp orange curaçao
½ tsp maraschino liqueur
1 dash bitters
ice cubes
Garnish: twist of orange

Shake the ingredients with ice and strain into a chilled cocktail glass. Garnish with the twist of orange.

FRUITY IRISHMAN

45ml (1½oz) Bailey's Irish Cream

22ml (¾oz) Midori

ice cubes

Stir the ingredients with ice in a lowball glass and serve.

Cinco de Mayo

'Here's to the lady dressed in black, once she walks by she never looks back, and when she kisses, oh how sweet, she makes things stand that never had feet.'

SANGRIA

1 orange, lemon and lime

1 bottle dry red or white wine

1 quart club soda

1 tbsp sugar

(Optional additions: 30ml (1oz) brandy, 30ml (1oz) triple sec and pineapple slices or maraschino cherries)

Slice the fruits and combine these with the wine and sugar (include the other options, if used). Refrigerate overnight. Mix with the club soda just before serving.

Valentine's Day

'Here's to one and only one, and may that one be thee. Who loves but one and only one, and may that one be me.'

LOVE POTION

45ml (1½oz) orange vodka

22ml (¾oz) Chambord

22ml (¾oz) cranberry juice

ice cubes

Shake the ingredients with ice and strain into a chilled cocktail glass.

Labor Day

'Here's to prosperity...
and the wisdom to use it well.'

VELVET HAMMER

45ml (1½oz) vodka

15ml (½oz) white crème de cacao

1 splash half and half

ice cubes

Shake the ingredients with ice, strain into a chilled cocktail glass and serve ungarnished.

Easter

*'Father of fathers, make me one,
a fit example for a son.'*

EASTER EGG

30ml (1oz) rum

30ml (1oz) apricot brandy

1 splash pineapple juice

1 splash apple juice

ice cubes

Garnish: orange wheel and maraschino cherry

Shake the ingredients with ice and pour the mixture over fresh ice cubes in a Collins glass. Serve garnished with a flag.

Easter Egg

4th of July

'May the roof above us never fall in, and may the friends gathered below it never fall out.'

FIRECRACKER

30ml (1oz) cinnamon or peppermint schnapps

2–3 drops Tabasco sauce

1 dash grenadine

1 splash club soda

Build the ingredients, in the order given, in a shot glass. Place a paper napkin over the glass, slam, and drink it while still foaming.

Halloween

*'May those who live truly be always believed,
and those who deceive us be always deceived.'*

SWAMP WATER

37ml (1¼oz) green Chartreuse

37ml (1¼oz) pineapple juice

37ml (1¼oz) lime juice

ice cubes

Build the ingredients over ice in a highball glass.

Weddings

'Here's to the wings of love, may they never moult a feather, till your little shoes and my big boots, are under the bed together.'

ZOMBIE

60ml (2oz) light rum

30ml (1oz) dark rum

30ml (1oz) apricot brandy

1 splash simple syrup

1 splash pineapple juice

1 splash 151 rum

ice cubes

Shake the rums, except the 151 rum, brandy, simple syrup and pineapple juice with ice. Pour into a Collins or hurricane glass and float a layer of the 151 on top.

WEREWOLF

30ml (1oz) Drambuie

30ml (1oz) bourbon

ice cubes

Build over ice in a rocks glass.

WEDDING BELLE COCKTAIL

22ml (¾oz) Dubonnet

22ml (¾oz) gin

1 splash cherry brandy

1 splash orange juice

ice cubes

Shake the ingredients with ice and strain into a chilled cocktail glass. Serve ungarnished.

WEDDING CAKE

22ml (¾oz) gin

22ml (¾oz) amaretto

1 splash orange juice

1 splash pineapple juice

1 splash cream

ice cubes

Shake the ingredients with ice and strain over fresh ice cubes in a highball glass.

Christmas

'Here's to the holly with its bright red berry.
Here's to Christmas, let's make it merry.'

TOM & JERRY

30ml (1oz) brandy	
30ml (1oz) rum	
1 egg	
sugar	
cinnamon and allspice	
ground cloves	
hot milk or boiling water	
Garnish: nutmeg	

Batter: use one egg per serving. Separate the egg and beat the egg white until firm. Beat the yolk until it is very thin. Fold the white into the yolk and add the sugar (according to taste and consistency). Add a touch of cinnamon, allspice and ground cloves. Preheat your mugs with hot water. Put one tablespoon of the batter, brandy and rum into the mug. Top up the mug with very hot milk or boiling water, stirring gently. Sprinkle the top with a dusting of nutmeg.

YE OLDE WASSAIL

1 quart rum or brandy	
1 quart ale (or beer)	
120ml (4oz) powdered sugar	
3 eggs	
1 tbsp nutmeg	
1 tbsp ginger	
1 tbsp grated lemon peel	

Heat the ale (or beer) and spices to almost boiling. Beat the eggs with the sugar, while the ale is still heating up. Combine both in a large pitcher. Put the rum (or brandy) in another large pitcher and turn from one to another until mixed well. Then pour the mixture into a holiday wreathed wassail bowl (or punch bowl). This drink is best served hot.

POINSETTIA

7ml (¼oz) triple sec	
1 splash cranberry juice	
champagne (to fill)	
Garnish: twist of lemon	

Combine the ingredients in a champagne glass. Garnish with the twist of lemon.

EGGNOG

24 eggs (separate yolks from egg whites)

2 cups sugar

1 quart bourbon

2 cups brandy

1 quart heavy cream

2 quarts milk

1 quart vanilla ice cream

Garnish: nutmeg

In a punch or large bowl, beat the egg yolks and sugar until thick. Add the bourbon and brandy, and stir. Add the cream and milk, and whip. Break up the ice cream and add, stirring well. Beat the egg whites until stiff and fold into the mixture. Refrigerate for at least an hour before serving. When ready to serve, pour into a highball glass and sprinkle nutmeg on top.

Eggnog

MULLED WINE

3x750ml (25oz) bottles of wine

½ tsp nutmeg

½ tsp cinnamon

½ tsp powdered clove

2 tbsp cloves

juice of 1 orange

honey or brown sugar to taste

In a large saucepan over a very low heat, combine the ingredients and heat until sufficiently warm – be careful not to overheat. Serve in a mug.

FROZEN DRINKS

Frozen cocktails offer the most creativity in presentation. These are either ice or ice-cream based, and can be topped with whipped cream, garnished with a variety of fruits, sugars, candies, edible flowers, etc. The sky is the limit as long as you remember to garnish with a complimentary flavour. Because of their size, frozen drinks have a lower alcohol content. They are often enjoyed during the hot summer months. However, don't let their refreshing values fool you into thinking that you can drink as much of them as you want, especially in the hot sun.

Frozen drinks are popular also because of their usual sweetness, which makes them a good choice for an after-dinner drink. Crushed or cubed ice can be used in these recipes. If your blender can't crush ice cubes, use crushed or shaved ice.

WAHINE

15ml (½ oz) lemon juice	
45ml (1½ oz) pineapple juice (unsweetened)	
30ml (1oz) light rum	
30ml (1oz) vodka	
7ml (¼ oz) simple syrup	
shaved ice	
Garnish: sprig of mint and fresh fruit	

Blend the ingredients with one scoop of shaved ice. Pour the mixture into a decorative mug or coconut shell. Garnish with the sprig of mint and fresh fruit.

CHI-CHI

30ml (1oz) vodka	
1 splash cream of coconut	
1 splash pineapple juice	
1 splash half and half	
cubed or crushed ice	
Garnish: fresh pineapple	

Blend the ingredients with ice until smooth and pour the mixture into a hurricane glass. Garnish with the fresh pineapple.

STRAWBERRY MARGARITA

30ml (1oz) tequila	
15ml (½ oz) triple sec	
1 splash puréed strawberries (or mash fresh strawberries)	
1 splash sour mix	
1 dash grenadine	
cubed or crushed ice	
Garnish: strawberry and lime wedge	

Blend the ingredients with the ice until smooth and pour into a sugar-frosted, decorative glass. Garnish with the lime wedge and the strawberry.

HUMMER

30ml (1oz) Kahlúa

30ml (1oz) rum

2 scoops ice cream

whipped cream (optional)

Blend the ingredients until smooth and serve in a large parfait glass. Top with whipped cream, if desired.

E PLURIBUS UNUM

22ml (¾oz) Frangelico

22ml (¾oz) Chambord

22ml (¾oz) Kahlúa

2 scoops chocolate ice cream

whipped cream (optional)

Garnish: white chocolate

Blend the ingredients until smooth and serve in a large parfait glass. Float a layer of whipped cream on top, if desired. Garnish with shavings of white chocolate.

JAGUAR

60ml (2oz) Galliano

30ml (1oz) white crème de cacao

2 scoops ice cream

whipped cream (optional)

Blend the ingredients until smooth and serve in a large parfait glass. Top with whipped cream, if desired.

CORAL REEF

45ml (1½oz) vodka

60ml (2oz) Malibu or CocoRibe

6 strawberries or 1 tbsp (15ml) strawberry preserve

crushed ice

Blend the ingredients with ice until smooth. Serve ungarnished in a chilled wine goblet.

SON OF A PEACH

37ml (1¼oz) peach brandy

1 splash sour mix

1 splash pineapple juice

cubed or crushed ice

Blend the ingredients with ice until smooth and serve in a hurricane or large, decorative glass.

Mudslide

Blend the first five ingredients together until smooth. Circle a drizzle of chocolate syrup in a large parfait glass. Pour in the ingredients and top with the whipped cream and another drizzle of chocolate syrup.

KAT'S KISS

30ml (1oz) crème de noyaux

30ml (1oz) Bailey's Irish Cream

2 scoops ice cream

whipped cream (optional)

Blend the ingredients until smooth and serve in a large parfait glass. Top with whipped cream, if desired.

MUDSLIDE

30ml (1oz) Kahlúa

30ml (1oz) vodka

30ml (1oz) Bailey's Irish Cream

2 scoops vanilla ice cream

1 Oreo cookie

chocolate syrup

whipped cream

SAUZALIKY

30ml (1oz) tequila

1 splash orange juice

1 dash lemon juice

half a banana

cubed or crushed ice

Blend the ingredients with ice until smooth. Serve in a highball glass.

Koala Bear

KOALA BEAR

30ml (1oz) crème de banane

30ml (1oz) dark crème
de cacao

2 scoops vanilla ice cream

whipped cream (optional)

Garnish: nutmeg

*Blend the ingredients until smooth
and serve in a large parfait glass.
Top with whipped cream, if desired.
Sprinkle a dusting of nutmeg on top.*

BANANA BARBADOS

22ml (¾oz) Mount Gay Eclipse

22ml (¾oz) Myers's rum

15ml (½oz) crème de banane

1 large splash sour mix

2 scoops vanilla ice cream

*Blend the ingredients and pour
the mixture into a hurricane
glass. Float a dash of Myers's
on top.*

STRAWBERRY SMASH

30ml (1oz) Bacardi light rum

30ml (1oz) wilderberry
schnapps

15ml (½oz) 151 rum

30ml (1oz) sour mix

1 cup strawberries

1 banana

cubed or crushed ice

*Blend the ingredients with the ice
until smooth and serve in a
hurricane glass. Garnish with a
fresh strawberry.*

DIZZY DAISY

37ml (1¼oz) vodka

22ml (¾oz) crème de banane

22ml (¾oz) puréed strawberries

22ml (¾oz) half and half

whipped cream (optional)

Garnish: fresh fruit and
chocolate syrup

*Blend the ingredients together until
smooth and serve in a large parfait
glass. Top with whipped cream,
if desired. Serve garnished
with the fresh fruit. Finish
with a drizzle of choco-
late syrup over the fruit.*

BLUE HAWAIIAN

30ml (1oz) blue curaçao

30ml (1oz) rum

1 splash cream of coconut

1 splash pineapple juice

crushed ice

Garnish: pineapple wedge
and maraschino cherry

*Blend the ingredients until smooth
and pour into in a highball glass.
Spear the cherry and pineapple
wedge and decorate the drink.*

COOKIE CRUSHER

30ml (1oz) white crème
de menthe

30ml (1oz) dark crème de cacao

2 scoops ice cream

1 Oreo cookie

whipped cream (optional)

*Blend the ingredients until smooth
and serve in a large parfait glass.
Top with whipped cream, if desired.*

FROZEN FRUIT DAIQUIRI

37ml (1¼oz) rum

37ml (1¼oz) sour mix

1 splash simple syrup

fresh fruit, fruit juice or puréed
fruit (of your choice)

crushed ice

whipped cream

Garnish: lime wedge

*Blend the ingredients with ice until
smooth and serve in a hurricane
glass. Top with the whipped cream
and garnish with the lime wedge.*

DEATH BY CHOCOLATE

30ml (1oz) dark crème de cacao

30ml (1oz) Kahlúa

30ml (1oz) vodka

30ml (1oz) chocolate syrup

2 scoops chocolate ice cream

whipped cream (optional)

Garnish: maraschino cherry

*Blend the ingredients until smooth
and serve in a large parfait glass.
Top with whipped cream, if
desired. Garnish with
the cherry.*

CALYPSO DAIQUIRI

37ml (1¼oz) Myers's rum cream

15ml (2 ½oz) sour mix

15ml (½oz) half and half

1 banana

1 tsp vanilla extract

cubed or crushed ice

Garnish: orange wheel and maraschino cherry

Blend the ingredients with ice until smooth and pour into a hurricane glass. Decorate with a flag.

CHOCOLATE ALMOND KISS

15ml (½oz) Frangelico

15ml (½oz) dark crème de cacao

15ml (½oz) vodka

2 scoops ice cream

whipped cream (optional)

Garnish: chocolate sprinkles

Blend the ingredients until smooth and serve in a large parfait glass. Decorate with whipped cream, if desired. Garnish with the chocolate sprinkles.

RASPBERRY COLADA

30ml (1oz) Chambord

30ml (1oz) rum

1 splash piña colada mix

ice cubes

Garnish: fresh fruit

Blend the ingredients with ice until smooth and pour into a hurricane glass. Garnish with the fresh fruit.

FROZEN ALMOND JOY

22ml (¾oz) rum

22ml (¾oz) amaretto

22ml (¾oz) Kahlúa

22ml (¾oz) dark crème de cacao

60ml (2oz) crème de coconut

2 scoops vanilla ice cream

chocolate syrup

whipped cream

Garnish: toasted coconut

Prepare large parfait glass by drizzling chocolate into it. Blend the spirits and crème de coconut with ice cream. Top with the whipped cream and garnish with the toasted coconut.

HOT DRINKS

Hot drinks are warming in the winter, a nice finish to a great meal, a perfect bedtime nightcap, or a great treat when just feeling 'blah'. The thing to remember when serving a hot drink is that it is indeed hot and you should be cautious while preparing and serving it. Although just about any mug will do, the traditional Irish coffee mug is the prettiest to use. If any other glass is used, make sure that it is heat resistant to avoid the explosion of hot liquid and glass.

CARIBBEAN COFFEE

30ml (1oz) dark rum

22ml (¾oz) Tia Maria

coffee (to fill)

whipped cream

Combine the spirits in a mug and fill with coffee. Top with the whipped cream.

KEOKI COFFEE

22ml (¾oz) brandy

22ml (¾oz) Kahlúa

coffee (to fill)

whipped cream

Garnish: maraschino cherry

Combine the spirits in a mug and fill with coffee. Top with the whipped cream and garnish with the cherry.

SWISS COFFEE

15ml (½oz) peppermint schnapps

15ml (½oz) dark crème de cacao

coffee (to fill)

whipped cream

Combine the spirits in a mug and fill with coffee. Float the whipped cream on top.

JAMAICAN COFFEE

30ml (1oz) Tia Maria

22ml (¾oz) rum

coffee (to fill)

whipped cream

Combine the spirits in a mug and fill with coffee. Top with the whipped cream.

THE BEACH WARMER

22ml (¾oz) Chambord

22ml (¾oz) Kahlúa

hot chocolate (to fill)

whipped cream

Combine the liqueurs in a mug and fill with hot chocolate. Top with the whipped cream.

MEXICAN COFFEE

22ml (¾oz) Kahlúa

22ml (¾oz) tequila

coffee (to fill)

whipped cream

Garnish: maraschino cherry

Combine the spirits in a mug and fill with coffee. Top with the whipped cream and garnish with the cherry.

SPANISH COFFEE

30ml (1oz) brandy

15ml (½oz) anisette

coffee (to fill)

whipped cream

Combine the spirits in a mug and fill with coffee. Float the whipped cream on top.

KOKO COFFEE

30ml (1oz) white crème de cacao

coffee (to fill)

whipped cream

Garnish: dark crème de cacao

Pour the white crème de cacao into a mug and add the coffee. Top with whipped cream and garnish with dribbles of dark crème de cacao.

MIDNIGHT MOZART

22ml (¾oz) Kahlúa

22ml (¾oz) Mozart

coffee (to fill)

whipped cream

Combine the liqueurs in a mug and fill with coffee. Float the whipped cream on top.

COFFEE BLAZER

15ml (½oz) Kahlúa

15ml (½oz) brandy

coffee (to fill)

whipped cream

Garnish: maraschino cherry

Combine the spirits in a mug and fill with coffee. Top with the whipped cream and garnish with the cherry.

ITALIAN COFFEE

37ml (1¼oz) amaretto

coffee (to fill)

whipped cream

Garnish: maraschino cherry

Pour the amaretto into a mug, add the coffee and top with the whipped cream. Garnish with the cherry.

HOT TODDY

37ml (1¼oz) brandy, bourbon (or any liquor of your choice)

1 tsp sugar

boiling water (to fill)

Garnish: twist of orange or lemon

In a mug, stir together the sugar and spirit. Top up with the hot water. Garnish with the twist of orange or lemon.

HOT NUTTY IRISHMAN

22ml (¾ oz) Frangelico

22ml (¾ oz) Bailey's Irish Cream

coffee (to fill)

whipped cream

Combine the liqueurs in a mug and fill with coffee. Float the whipped cream on top.

BLUE BLAZER

1 tbsp honey dissolved in half a mug of hot water and an equal amount of Scotch in a separate mug

Garnish: twist of lemon and nutmeg

Ignite the Scotch and carefully pour it back and forth between the two mugs until the flame goes out. Pour into a clean mug. Garnish with the twist of lemon and a sprinkle of nutmeg.

BLACK MONK

37ml (1¼ oz) B & B

coffee (to fill)

whipped cream

Sugar-rim an Irish coffee mug and pour the B & B and coffee into it. Top with the whipped cream.

Hot Buttered Rum

HOT BUTTERED RUM

60ml (2oz) rum

1 tsp sugar

1 cinnamon stick

1 clove

boiling cider (to fill)

1 tsp butter

Garnish: spiral of lemon peel

Stir the spices and rum in a mug and fill with cider. Garnish with the lemon peel. Float the butter on top.

IRISH COFFEE

1 jigger of Irish whiskey

2 tsp sugar

hot coffee (to fill)

fresh cream

Rinse a glass with boiling water, so it is hot to start with. Add the whiskey, sugar and coffee, and stir. Using the back of a spoon, slowly pour the cream so that it floats on top of the mixture. Do not stir the cream into the coffee. Traditionally, this is best sipped through the cream. The fresher the cream you use, the better it tastes, too.

Irish Coffee is indeed Irish in origin. The port of Foynes, located in County Limerick, was a major hub for air traffic between the United States of America and Europe during the 1930s and 1940s. In 1943, one transatlantic flight encountered some really bad weather and was forced to turn back to Foynes. The weather was just as bad upon their return, so the passengers headed towards the terminal restaurant. Realizing how miserable these passengers were, Chef Joe Sheridan grabbed a bottle of Irish whiskey and prepared some comforting drinks for them. Legend has it that one of the passengers asked, 'is this Brazilian coffee?' to which Sheridan answered, 'No, that's Irish Coffee!'

CAFÉ ALPINE

30ml (1oz) peppermint
schnapps

coffee (to fill)

whipped cream

*Mix the coffee and schnapps in a
mug and top with the whipped cream.*

HUNTERS COFFEE

15ml (½oz) Tia Maria

15ml (½oz) Grand Marnier

coffee (to fill)

whipped cream

Garnish: maraschino cherry

*Combine the liqueurs in a mug and
fill with coffee. Top with the whipped
cream and garnish with the cherry.*

CAFÉ ROYALE

coffee

brandy

1 sugar cube

*In a mug, float a layer of brandy on
the coffee. Place the sugar cube on
a spoon, soak it in brandy and
ignite. Lower the flaming spoon into
the mug slowly, igniting the brandy.
Stir gently and serve when the
flame dies out.*

CAFÉ GATES

15ml (½oz) Tia Maria

15ml (½oz) Grand Marnier

15ml (½oz) dark crème de cacao

coffee (to fill)

whipped cream

*Combine the liqueurs in a mug and
fill with the coffee. Float the whipped
cream on top.*

ENGLISH COFFEE

15ml (½oz) Kahlúa

15ml (½oz) amaretto

15ml (½oz) Tia Maria

15ml (½oz) dark crème
de cacao

coffee (to fill)

whipped cream

*Combine the liqueurs in a mug
and fill with coffee. Float the
whipped cream on top.*

MOCKTAILS

The term 'mocktails' is a combination of the words 'mock', which means to imitate, and cocktail. These drinks resemble cocktails but are nonalcoholic or very low in alcohol content. Some bartenders resent having to mix these drinks, considering it a waste because they don't contain spirits. However, one must consider that these drinks are usually intended for persons not old enough to drink, a recovering alcoholic or someone on medication and, my personal favourite, a designated driver. So, take the time to make these drinks and serve them with pleasure.

TRANSFUSION

90ml (3oz) grape juice

180ml (6oz) ginger ale

1 splash lime juice

ice cubes

Garnish: lime wedge

Build the ingredients over ice in a tall glass. Garnish with the lime wedge.

MONTEGO BAY

60ml (2oz) orange juice

60ml (2oz) sour mix

1 splash grenadine

club soda (to fill)

ice cubes

Garnish: fresh fruit

Shake all the ingredients, except the soda, with ice. Pour into a tall glass and top up with the soda. Garnish with a flag of fresh fruit.

LIME FREEZE

90ml (3oz) lime juice

2 scoops lime sherbert

Garnish: lime wedge

Blend the ingredients until smooth. Serve in a large parfait glass. Garnish with the lime wedge.

CRANBERRY COOLER

cranberry juice

1 splash club soda

Garnish: lime wheel

Build the ingredients in a highball glass. Garnish with the lime wheel.

Cranberry Cooler

TOOTS

60ml (2oz) orange soda

1 scoop orange sherbet

1 scoop chocolate ice cream

whipped cream

Garnish: orange wedge

*Blend the ingredients until smooth
and pour into a hurricane glass. Top
with the whipped cream and garnish
with the orange wedge.*

SAN FRANCISCO

Equal parts of pineapple,
orange and grapefruit juice
and sour mix

2 dashes grenadine

club soda (to fill)

ice cubes

*Shake all the ingredients, except the
soda, with ice. Strain into a goblet
and top up with the soda.*

APRÈS TENNIS BRACER

⅓ part orange juice

⅔ ice cubes

Garnish: orange wheel

*Build the ingredients over ice in a
Collins glass. Garnish with the
orange wheel.*

LEMON SQUASH

lemon wedges

1 splash simple syrup

club soda (to fill)

ice cubes

*Muddle the lemon wedges with the
syrup in a highball glass. Add the ice
and top up with the soda.*

KIDDY COCKTAIL

1 splash grenadine

1 splash sour mix

ice cubes

Garnish: orange wheel and
maraschino cherry

*Shake the ingredients with ice and
serve in a highball glass. Garnish
with a flag.*

CREAMSICLE

120ml (4oz) orange juice

2 scoops ice cream

whipped cream

Garnish: orange wheel (optional)

*Blend the ingredients and serve in
a tall glass. Top with the whipped
cream and garnish with the orange
wheel, if desired.*

SHIRLEY TEMPLE

1 splash grenadine

lemon-lime soda (to fill)

ice cubes

Garnish: orange wheel and
maraschino cherry

*Build the ingredients over ice in a
highball glass. Garnish with a flag.*

ROSY PIPPIN

120ml (4oz) apple juice

1 splash grenadine

1 splash sour mix

ginger ale (to fill)

ice cubes

Garnish: apple slice

*Shake the apple juice, grenadine and
sour mix with ice. Pour into a
Collins glass. Top up with the ginger
ale and garnish with the apple slice.*

Shirley Temple

MIAMI VICE

60ml (2oz) half and half

60ml (2oz) root beer

1 splash chocolate syrup

cola (to fill)

ice cubes

*Shake all the ingredients, except the
cola, with ice. Pour into a tall glass
and top up with the cola.*

JOGGER

1 splash lime juice

club soda (to fill)

ice cubes

Garnish: lime wedge

*Build the ingredients over ice in a
highball glass. Garnish with the
lime wedge.*

BLACK COW

root beer

2 scoops vanilla ice cream

whipped cream

Garnish: maraschino cherry (optional)

Pour the root beer slowly over the ice cream in a large parfait glass. Top with the whipped cream and garnish with the cherry, if desired.

Black Cow

MARGARITA

60ml (2oz) sour mix

1 splash lime juice

1 splash orange juice

ice cubes

Garnish: lime wedge

Blend the ingredients with ice. Serve in a salt-rimmed margarita glass. Garnish with the lime wedge.

SUNSET COOLER

120ml (4oz) cranberry juice

75ml (2½oz) orange juice

1 splash lemon juice

ginger ale (to fill)

ice cubes

Garnish: fresh fruit

Blend the juices with ice and pour into a Collins glass. Top up with the ginger ale. Garnish with a flag of fresh fruit.

DOWN EAST DELIGHT

Equal parts of cranberry, pineapple and orange juice

1 dash simple syrup

ice cubes

Garnish: maraschino cherry

Build the ingredients over ice in a Collins glass. Garnish with the cherry.

ROSIE'S SPECIAL

Equal parts of tea and
orange juice

1 splash club soda

ice cubes

Garnish: maraschino cherry

*Build the ingredients over ice in a
Collins glass. Garnish with the cherry.*

JOHNNY APPLESEED

60ml (2oz) apple juice

1 splash orange juice

1 splash club soda

ice cubes

*Blend the ingredients with ice until
smooth. Serve in a champagne glass.*

STRAWBERRY
ORANGEANA

90ml (3oz) orange juice

60ml (2oz) fresh or frozen
strawberries

1 banana

ice cubes

Garnish: fresh fruit

*Blend the ingredients with ice until
smooth and pour into a large parfait glass. Garnish with a flag of
fresh fruit.*

PONY'S NECK

1 dash lime juice

2 dashes bitters

ginger ale (to fill)

ice cubes

Garnish: twist of lemon and
maraschino cherry

*Build the ingredients over ice in a
highball glass. Garnish with the twist
of lemon and the cherry.*

UNFUZZY NAVEL

90ml (3oz) orange juice

1 fresh peach or nectarine
(cut into chunks)

1 dash grenadine

ice cubes

*Blend the ingredients with ice until
smooth. Serve in a highball glass.*

SCHNOOKIE BROOKIE

90ml (3oz) orange juice

90ml (3oz) club soda

1 scoop ice cream

Garnish: maraschino cherry

*Blend the ingredients until smooth
and pour the mixture into a hurricane glass. Garnish with the cherry.*

WHAT ME WORRY?

1 glass nonalcoholic beer

1 splash tomato juice or
Bloody Mary mix

Garnish: lime wedge

*Combine the ingredients in a mug
and garnish with the lime wedge.*

CINDERELLA

Equal parts of orange and
pineapple juice

1 dash grenadine

1 splash club soda

1 splash sour mix

Garnish: maraschino cherry

*Shake all the ingredients together,
except the soda, and pour into a
Collins glass. Top up with the soda
and garnish with the cherry.*

I'LL FAKE MANHATTAN

45ml (1½oz) cranberry juice

45ml (1½oz) orange juice

2 dashes orange bitters

1 dash grenadine

1 dash lemon juice

ice cubes

*Stir the ingredients with ice and
strain into a chilled cocktail glass.*

A.S. MACPHERSON

3–4 dashes bitters

1 splash sour mix

1 splash orange juice

club soda (to fill)

ice cubes

Garnish: fresh fruit

*Shake all the ingredients, except the
soda, with ice. Strain into a Collins
glass over fresh ice. Top up with the
soda and decorate with a flag.*

PEARLS AND LACE

60ml (2oz) orange soda

60ml (2oz) cola

60ml (2oz) root beer

60ml (2oz) 7-Up

1 splash lemonade

ice cubes

Build over ice in a tall glass.

CARDINAL PUNCHLESS

Equal parts of cranberry juice
and ginger ale

1 splash orange juice

1 dash lemon juice

1 dash simple syrup

ice cubes

Build over ice in a Collins glass.

VIRGIN PIÑA COLADA

90ml (3oz) pineapple juice

60ml (2oz) cream of coconut

ice cubes

whipped cream

Garnish: pineapple wedge and maraschino cherry

Blend the ingredients with ice until smooth. Serve in a hurricane glass. Garnish with the pineapple and cherry.

Virgin Piña Colada

TOMATO COOLER

1 splash lemon juice

tomato juice (to fill)

1 splash tonic

Garnish: lime wedge and celery stalk

Combine the lemon and tomato juice in a tall glass. Add the tonic and garnish with the lemon wedge and celery stalk.

NICHOLAS

1 splash grapefruit juice

1 splash orange juice

1 splash sour mix

1 dash grenadine

ice cubes

Shake all the ingredients together and pour over ice in a highball glass. Serve ungarnished.

HONEYMOON COCKTAIL

1 part apple juice

1 part orange juice

1 squeeze of lime juice

2 tsp honey

crushed ice

Garnish: 2 spirals of orange peel and 2 sugared cherries

Place three spoons of crushed ice in a cocktail shaker. Add the apple and orange juice, the lime juice and the honey. Shake well, then strain the mixture into two champagne flutes. Garnish with the spirals of orange peel and the cherries. Serve in bed.

GRENADINE RICKEY

45ml (1½oz) grenadine

45ml (1½oz) lime juice

45ml (1½oz) club soda

ice cubes

Garnish: lime wedge

Combine the grenadine and lime juice with ice in a highball glass. Top up with the soda. Garnish with the lime wedge.

FRUIT SMOOTHIE

180ml (6oz) orange juice

1 cup fresh fruit (of your choice)

1 banana

1 scoop ice

Blend all the ingredients until smooth. Serve in a hurricane glass.

Fruit Smoothie

ROY ROGERS

cola (to fill)

1 splash grenadine

ice cubes

Garnish: orange wheel and
maraschino cherry

*Build the ingredients over ice in
a highball glass and garnish with
a flag.*

STRAWBERRY COLADA

Equal parts of fresh or frozen
strawberries, cream of coconut
and pineapple juice

ice cubes

Garnish: fresh fruit

*Blend the ingredients with ice until
smooth. Serve in a hurricane glass
and garnish with a flag of fresh fruit.*

ORANGEADE

Equal parts of orange juice
and club soda

1 splash simple syrup

ice cubes

Garnish: orange wheel

*Build over ice in a highball glass and
garnish with the orange wheel.*

SONOMA NOUVEAU

150ml (5oz) nonalcoholic
white wine

club soda

cranberry juice

ice cubes

Garnish: twist of lemon

*Pour the wine over ice in a Collins
glass and add the soda to almost
full. Float the cranberry juice on top
and garnish with the twist of lemon.*

PAC MAN

1 dash bitters

1 dash grenadine

1 splash lemon juice

ginger ale (to fill)

ice cubes

Garnish: orange wheel

*Stir all the ingredients, except the
ginger ale, with ice. Pour into a highball glass and fill with the ginger ale.
Garnish with the orange wheel.*

PMS

Equal parts of cranberry and
orange juice

ice cubes

Build over ice in a highball glass.

VIRGIN MARY

Salt, pepper and celery salt
to taste

1 dash Worcestershire sauce

1 dash Tabasco sauce

1 dash lime juice

180ml (6oz) tomato juice

ice cubes

Garnish: celery stalk and
lime wedge

*Starting with the spices, build the
ingredients in a tall, iced-filled glass.
Garnish with the celery stalk and
lime wedge.*

PINK LASSIE

60ml (2oz) cranberry juice

30ml (1oz) pineapple juice

30ml (1oz) simple syrup

1 splash club soda

1 scoop ice cream

*Blend the ingredients until smooth.
Serve in a champagne flute.*

MISSIONARY

60ml (2oz) pineapple juice

30ml (1oz) simple syrup

30ml (1oz) sour mix

ice cubes

Garnish: pineapple wedge and
maraschino cherry (optional)

*Shake all the ingredients together
and serve over ice in a highball
glass. Garnish with the pineapple
wedge, or a flag if preferred.*

STRAWBERRY DAIQUIRI (VIRGIN)

90ml (3oz) fresh or frozen
strawberries

1 splash sour mix

1 dash grenadine

ice cubes

Garnish: fresh fruit

*Blend the ingredients with ice until
smooth. Serve in a hurricane glass
and garnish with a flag of fruit.*

SAGINAW SNOOZE

90ml (3oz) apple juice

90ml (3oz) cranberry juice

1 tsp honey

Garnish: lemon wheel and
cinnamon stick

*Heat the ingredients together and
pour into an Irish coffee mug.
Garnish with the lemon wheel and
cinnamon stick.*

BEACH BLANKET BINGO

Equal parts of cranberry and grapefruit juice

club soda (to fill)

ice cubes

Garnish: lime wedge

Stir the juices with ice in a Collins glass and top up with the soda. Garnish with the lime wedge.

SAFE SEX ON THE BEACH

1 part peach nectar

3 parts pineapple juice

3 parts orange juice

1 squeeze of fresh lime juice

ice cubes

Garnish: twist of lime, slice of kiwi fruit and a strawberry

Place four ice cubes in a cocktail mixing glass and add the peach nectar (usually a blend of peach juice with other, deflavoured fruit juice bases), pineapple juice, orange juice and the squeeze of lime juice. Stir it well and strain into a tall glass. Add fresh ice and garnish with the twist of lime, slice of kiwi fruit and the strawberry.

Safe Sex on the Beach

LIME COLA

1 splash lime juice

cola (to fill)

ice cubes

Garnish: lime wedge

Build the ingredients over ice in a tall glass. Garnish with the lime wedge.

GLOSSARY

AGE The time a spirit is left to mature before bottling it.

APÉRITIF A drink that is served before dinner to stimulate the appetite.

BACK A nonalcoholic drink, or a small glass of beer served with a shot of liquor.

BAR BACK The bartender's assistant who is usually responsible for filling the ice buckets, stocking beer and helping with other mundane chores.

BASE LIQUOR The main ingredient in a drink.

BITTERS An additive made from bark, herbs, roots and berries, which gives a bitter zest to drinks.

CALL A brand-name liquor that is a step above well and a notch below premium or top shelf.

CORDIAL Same as a liqueur; it's a sweet drink made from berries, fruit or herbs.

DASH A few of drops splashed into the glass. You can buy a dash bottle to get an exact measurement.

FLAG A garnish for a drink made with a skewered orange slice and maraschino cherry or other fresh fruit. Also, the term used when someone has had enough to drink.

FLAME A drink is topped with high-proof alcohol and ignited.

FROZEN A drink is blended in an electric blender with crushed ice or ice cream.

HALF AND HALF Equal parts of cream and milk.

LIQUEUR Same as a cordial. It's a sweet drink made from berries, fruit or herbs.

MIST To pour a straight alcoholic liquor over crushed ice.

NEAT A drink served at room temperature with no ice. Also a drink served without any mixer.

ON THE ROCKS A drink that is served over ice.

PONY 30ml (one-ounce) measure or a term for a small, stemmed flute glass.

PREMIUM A step above a call spirit, but not top shelf.

PROOF The alcohol content of a spirit.

SPLASH A small amount of mixer added to a drink.

STRAIGHT UP A drink mixed with ice and then strained into a glass.

STRAIN After shaking or stirring a drink with ice or fruit pulp, you usually want to separate it from the the liquid. Strainers usually fit over their containers, which allows you to do this.

SWIZZLE STICK A stick or straw, generally plastic, that is placed in the drink for stirring and serves as a decoration.

TOP SHELF The best or most costly spirits available.

TWIST The long piece of lemon, orange or lime peel that is twisted to release the oil from the zest layer, then dropped into the drink as a garnish.

UP A drink served with no ice. The glass may be chilled.

VIRGIN A nonalcoholic drink.

WEDGE A piece of fruit cut in half, and sliced again to garnish a drink.

WELL Bar stock spirits that are the lowest in cost.

CONVERSIONS

These measurements are not the exact mathematical equivalents, but are close and easiest to use. Remember mixology is an art, not a science.

TERM	METRIC	STANDARD
Dash	1ml	$\frac{1}{32}$ oz
Teaspoon	5ml	$\frac{1}{8}$ oz
Tablespoon	15ml	$\frac{1}{2}$ oz
Splash	15ml	$\frac{1}{2}$ oz
Pony	30ml	1oz
Jigger	45ml	1$\frac{1}{2}$ oz
Split	180ml	6oz
Pint	480ml	16oz
Fifth	750ml	26oz
Quart	960ml	32oz

DENSITIES

Different liqueurs have different weights. In building a layered drink, the heaviest spirits should be poured first. Below is a basic chart, listing from heaviest to the lightest. Note that each brand will vary in density and it is best to experiment beforehand.

1 Crème de Cassis
2 Grenadine
3 Anisette
4 Crème de Noyeaux
5 Coffee Liqueur
6 Crème de Banane
7 Crème de Cacao
8 Crème de Menthe
9 Chambord
10 Blue Curaçao
11 Galliano
12 Amaretto
13 Tia Maria
14 Triple Sec
15 Drambuie
16 Frangelico
17 Orange Curaçao
18 Cinnamon Schnapps
19 Sambuca
20 Apricot Brandy
21 Blackberry Brandy
22 Cherry Brandy
23 Peach Brandy
24 Limoncello
25 Yellow Chartreuse
26 Midori
27 Bailey's Irish Cream
28 Sloe Gin
29 Cointreau
30 Grand Marnier
31 Peppermint Schnapps
32 B & B
33 Tuaca
34 Green Chartreuse
35 Southern Comfort
36 Pernod
37 Kirschwasser

GENERAL INDEX

DRINKS INDEX

251

253

254

AUTHOR DEDICATION

I'd like to dedicate this book to my dad for introducing me to the pleasure of drinking, and to my mom for the great example of drinking in moderation. Next, to my children who gave me good reason for a bit of libation here and there.

Thank you to Mr. G's Lounge for employing me for so long, Patsy and Johnn-O at Daly's for testing recipes, and cocktails.about.com, where I've written articles since 1997. Steve Visakay, Dale DeGroff, Gary Regan, Cheryl Charming, Lisa Shea, and Rod Santillanes for their support and friendship. Thank you!

PICTURE CREDITS

All photographs copyright: **www.imagesofafrica.co.za** with the exception of the following photographers and/or their agencies: Photo Access p2–3, 8–9, 54, 60–62, 68; Magazine Features (Pty) Ltd p10; Photofest p12–13; Steve Visakay p70 (below), 71; Karla Kik p73.